Meadowlark
Economics

D0556562

Meadowlark Economics

Collected Essays on Ecology, Community, and Spirituality

JAMES EGGERT

Preface by Thich Nhat Hanh
Foreword by Bill McKibben

North Atlantic Books
Berkeley, California

Copyright © 2009 by James Eggert. All rights reserved. No portion of this book, except for brief review, may be reproduced, stored in a retrieval system, or transmitted in any form or by any means—electronic, mechanical, photocopying, recording, or otherwise—without the written permission of the publisher. For information contact North Atlantic Books.

Published by
North Atlantic Books
P.O. Box 12327
Berkeley, California 94712

Cover art by James Huddle
Cover and book design by Jan Camp

Printed in the United States of America

Meadowlark Economics: Collected Essays on Ecology, Community, and Spirituality is sponsored by the Society for the Study of Native Arts and Sciences, a nonprofit educational corporation whose goals are to develop an educational and cross-cultural perspective linking various scientific, social, and artistic fields; to nurture a holistic view of arts, sciences, humanities, and healing; and to publish and distribute literature on the relationship of mind, body, and nature.

North Atlantic Books' publications are available through most bookstores. For further information, call 800-733-3000 or visit our website at www.northatlanticbooks.com.

Library of Congress Cataloging-in-Publication Data

Eggert, Jim, 1943–
Meadowlark economics : collected essays on ecology, economics, and spirituality / James Eggert ; foreword by Bill McKibben ; afterword by Thich Nhat Hanh.
    p. cm.
Rev. ed. of: Meadowlark economics : perspectives on ecology, work, and learning. 1992.
  Includes bibliographical references.
  ISBN 978-1-55643-767-0
  1. Economic development—Environmental aspects. 2. Environmental policy.
  3. Environmental protection. 4. Human ecology. 5. Environmental economics.
  I. Title.
HD75.6.E35 2008
363.7--dc22

2008039621

1 2 3 4 5 6 7 8 9 Sheridan 14 13 12 11 10 09

To my father, the late Robert J. Eggert,
who had a passion for learning

Grateful acknowledgment to the following publishers as sources of this collection: Ten Speed Press, (*Song of the Meadowlark,* 1999) for the essays "Meadowlark Economics," "Topsoil Drama," "A Passion for Learning," "High Jumping," "A Compensatory Ethic," "An Ideal Boss," "Craftsmanship and Salvation," "Simplify, Simplify: Henry Thoreau as Economic Prophet," "Ford's Mustangs and Darwin's Finches," and "A Cosmic Journey," as well as Bill McKibben's original foreword.

"Wal-Mart Pond" was originally published in the *Washington Post* Outlook Section while "Then the Sun Came Up: Creation Myths and Mr. Darwin" was published in the journal *Religious Humanism* under the title "The Creationists' Truth."

From Humanics Trade Group (*Wonder of the Tao,* 2004), I added the following essays: "What's Wrong with Capitalism?," "Life!," "Co-Responsibility," and "Like a Flower: A Meditation on Balance" (originally titled "The Wonder of the Tao"), as well as Thich Nhat Hanh's preface (originally *Wonder of the Tao*'s foreword). All essays have been revised and updated.

Grateful acknowledgment and a warm thank you to my project editor Elizabeth Kennedy and copyeditor Anne Connolly.

TABLE OF CONTENTS

Preface by Thich Nhat Hanh   ix
Foreword by Bill McKibben   xi

Part I: MEADOWLARK VALUES   1

Chapter 1: Meadowlark Economics   3

Chapter 2: What's Wrong with Capitalism?   9

Chapter 3: A Compensatory Ethic   17

Chapter 4: Craftsmanship and Salvation   21

Chapter 5: An Ideal Boss   25

Chapter 6: A Passion for Learning   31

Chapter 7: Topsoil Drama   37

Chapter 8: High Jumping   43

Part II: HENRY THOREAU AND CHARLES DARWIN   49

Chapter 9: Simplify, Simplify:
Henry Thoreau as Economic Prophet   51

Chapter 10: Wal-Mart Pond   57

Chapter 11: Ford's Mustangs and Darwin's Finches   63

Chapter 12: Then the Sun Came Up:
Creation Myths and Mr. Darwin   69

Part III: ON COSMIC AND SPIRITUAL EVOLUTION   75

Chapter 13: Celebrating Our Cosmic Journey   77

Chapter 14: Life!   89

Chapter 15: Co-Responsibility   97

Chapter 16: Like a Flower: A Meditation on Balance   105

Endnotes   117

Index   123

About the Author   131

Preface

by Thich Nhat Hanh

James Eggert offers us an engaging and poetic meditation on responsibility and interbeing. On the east coast of the USA we have the Statue of Liberty. Perhaps we should consider erecting a statue of responsibility on the west coast to remind us of our responsibility to each other and to our precious earth. Compassionate living is cultivated on the ground of understanding. It is possible to contribute to reducing the violence and destruction in our world with our everyday actions.

A step taken in mindfulness, a gentle smile, is already an act of peace, an act of compassion. Understanding deeply our inseparable connectedness with the natural world, with the trees, the sunshine, and the fresh air, we will know how to protect and how to take care of our precious planet, our home.

Please enjoy this offering of our friend, James Eggert, as an invitation to enter a deep relationship with our home, the earth and all her creatures, and to cultivate our awakened wisdom to find harmony and balance.

Foreword

by Bill McKibben

This is an unusual and valuable book in many respects. Its author, of course, is an economist—but not one devoted to the prevailing theology of his profession. Economists mostly work with the dedication of beavers or bees toward the great goal of More. Growth, expansion, and acceleration are the sacred words of their creed. And they have been enormously successful; their faith has spread around the world, crowding out all other creeds.

And yet there is always something rather, well, dismal about the field. This comes, I think, from its disciples' firm determination to wall off certain questions. For instance, "what makes for happiness?" Or "how do I figure out what I want from life?" They can answer these only by pointing to our consumer behavior—we must want what we buy. But they must sense the tautological absurdity of that line of argument.

Now comes James Eggert, one of a small school of economists who has begun to think outside the box. And it is curious that he begins by examining a word long used by his tribe: value. He inscribes it— marvelously—with *real* meaning, instead of the stale and transactional definition to be found in the front of the Econ textbooks. "Their song is pleasing, their color and swoop-of-flight is enchanting." Suddenly we are using good old nouns and adjectives, the sweet and solid Anglo-Saxon words instead of the ponderous latinate syllables of the professional journals. These things are *valuable,* he insists. And if you assign them a value in your heart, then you are in a position to begin to assess other developments. The "efficiency," for instance, of the modern farm, which leaves no room for the meadowlarks to nest and fledge their young.

This book rambles inefficiently along—which is why it is a good and true book, full of things to talk about with your friends and family and with yourself. There are delightful discussions of craftsmanship, of high jumping, of topsoil, of many of the things that constitute a joyful and complete human life. The essays are lighthearted and smart, and never didactic.

Eggert's book will be of great use to all who read it. But it would be especially helpful—though subversive—to give it to anyone you know with the misfortune to have been born an economist. It will help them see that they've been focused on one small patch of the whole. It will help them see that there really is more to life.

PART I

Meadowlark
Values

Chapter 1

Meadowlark Economics

By the power of our imagination we can sense the future generations breathing with the rhythm of our own breath or feel them hovering like a cloud of witnesses. Sometimes I fancy that if I were to turn my head suddenly, I would glimpse them over my shoulder.

—Joanna Macy

Considering the problems we face in the dawning of our twenty-first century—and the slow evolution of values we're seeing in response—I often wonder about the competency and even relevancy of many contemporary economists.

This may seem like an odd comment coming from someone who has spent over thirty years teaching the subject. Indeed, I've defended my discipline's importance to my students and to others on countless occasions. So what is our unique contribution?

Economists' stock in trade includes the following: recognizing scarcity, helping to make choices, identifying trade-offs, marshaling the power of incentives, and making connections (that may not always be obvious) between the larger economy and one's own small, individual, economic world.

On the last point, I recall a class in the mid-1980s when a student asked what I meant by "making connections." That same day, nature fortuitously provided me with an interesting and unusual example. I told the students that I'd had trouble getting to school that morning because a couple of aspen trees near a dammed-up marshy area had been cut overnight and blocked the roadway into town.

"Now what," I asked, "did international trade and finance have to do with these downed trees and my morning's frustration?" Working it through, we concluded that indeed there may have been the following connections:

- Who cut the trees? Probably beaver.
- Why were they felling trees near the road? Overpopulation.
- Why were there too many beaver? No trapping that year.
- What happened to the beaver pelt market? Decreased sales in overseas markets.
- Why did sales decrease? Because of the high value of the U.S. dollar in the spring of 1985.

Some of the fun of teaching is thinking through such illustrations, examining the connective tissue of the Big Economy and world markets, then trying to see how it relates to little you and me. Indeed, most economists are trained to do this kind of analysis quite well.

So what is our shortcoming? I believe it is simply this: We economists have simply not gone far enough in expanding our understanding of ecological values.

Ecology. Note that the words "economics" and "ecology" have the same prefix—eco—from the Greek *oikos,* which literally means "household." The original definition of economics implied an understanding and careful stewardship of household resources, whereas ecology implied an understanding and appreciation of the interrelationships within nature's "household." I believe these two households are becoming more interdependent and their futures more and more intimately linked. When we fail to calculate ecological values or to see the connections, we pave the way for losses that are both unintended and unwanted. One example (on a small scale, to be sure) is occurring in our area, a dairy farming region of the upper Midwest. We are losing our meadowlarks!

Those of us who walk, bike, or jog along our rural roads enjoy the few meadowlarks that are left. Their song is pleasing, their color and swoop-of-flight enchanting. The complete disappearance of meadowlarks would, plain and simple, be ethically wrong, and would also diminish the quality and richness of our lives.

Why are we losing our meadowlarks? Most likely they are disappearing as a result of haylage, a modern method of haying. Farmers now tend to green-cut their hay much earlier in the spring for the purpose of maximizing feed value. Years ago, most farmers let their hay grow longer—perhaps two to three weeks longer—before cutting it. It was then dried and raked into windrows before baling. This method gave the field-nesting birds (such as the meadowlarks and bobolinks) time to establish a brood and fledge their young before the mower arrived on the scene.

Haylage in turn is an offshoot of improved farm "efficiency," of substituting machinery and fossil fuels for labor, and of minimizing time and costly rain delays that characterized the old cutting/drying/baling method. These changes took place with the blessings of agricultural economists, university researchers, and on down the line to government agencies. But in the meantime, who was valuing the meadowlarks?

Despite their sweet song, these birds have no voice economically or politically. They represent a "zero" within our conventional economic accounting system (we don't even buy birdseed or build birdhouses for meadowlarks). Their disappearance would not create even the tiniest ripple in the commerce department's spreadsheets that are supposed to measure our standard of living.

In truth, there are "meadowlark values" (as opposed to strict economic values) everywhere—in estuaries and sand dunes, in wetlands and woodlands, in native prairies and Panamanian rain forests. Quite probably the quality of your own life is, to some degree, dependent on these values. They are on every continent; they can be seen upstate and downstate. Just look around and you will find them (like our meadowlarks) on your road, or next door, or perhaps in your own backyard.

Meadowlark values are underrepresented in the clear-cutting of old-growth forests to maximize short-run profit, or when politicians try to open up the Arctic National Wildlife Refuge and additional offshore areas for oil and gas exploration. Meadowlark values were shortchanged when economists pointed out (quite correctly) that Exxon's massive oil spill in Alaska actually increased our gross domestic product, or GDP, by putting billions into the cleanup, thereby fattening paychecks as well as state and national income.

Perhaps it is time we economists begin to rethink our strict adherence to dollar and GDP values. We should not, of course, discard our old and valuable skills: recognizing scarcity, making efficient choices, respecting the power of incentives, and pointing out trade-offs. But perhaps we need to broaden ourselves into a new kind of economist—someone who can incorporate ecological thinking and ecological values with market thinking and market values—a true meadowlark economist, if you will.

I'm ashamed to admit that I took my first elementary class in ecology after teaching economics for more than two decades. I still have a ways to go. I am now beginning to appreciate some of the earlier economics writers who represent such new thinking: Ken Boulding, Hazel Henderson, Herman Daly, Lester Brown, Leopold Kohr, and E. F. Schumacher, to name a few.

In addition, I hope that more and more prominent economists of today will feel comfortable not only with traditional market/growth economics, but will also know something of ecology, will value the integrity of the environment along with the "bottom line;" will promote development, but will also protect the standard of living of the other organisms with whom we share the planet.

Perhaps future economists can devise, like environmental impact statements (EIS), what might be called GIS or "grandchild impact statements," making sure our kids and their kids will have sustainable quantities of biological and other resources, helping to preserve our soils and waters, our fisheries and forests, whales and bluebirds—even the tiny toads and butterflies—so that these entities will have their voices represented too.

So all you CEOs and National Association of Business Economists, you classical Marxists and free-market fundamentalists, and us teachers too: Let's dedicate ourselves to a new standard of—what?—of meadowlark economics, if you will, of protecting and sustaining for the future a larger, more expansive, and comprehensive set of durable values.

Chapter 2

What's Wrong with Capitalism?

Earth is a laboratory wherein Nature has laid before us the results of countless experiments. She speaks to us; now let us listen.

—E. O. Wilson

Despite its materialistic virtues, something's amiss in the Land of Capitalism. It's a quality or *force* that all too often violates the natural laws that normally ensure life's beauty and balance, its health and long-term continuity.

To search for that undermining force, let us pretend for a moment that you could literally pick up market capitalism as if it were a flawed gemstone. Now place it in the palm of your hand and, turning it over and over, inspect the gem for defects, fissures, and possible flaws. What would be the economist's perspective? Now angle it slightly differently; what would be the viewpoint of an ecologist? And finally, is it possible to look at our economy from a prairie's perspective, or that of an old growth forest?

Economist's Perspective

Economists do acknowledge capitalism's imperfections, often describing its defects as "market failures." These include the many unintended impacts ballooning beyond regular business costs into what economists call "externalities," where consumption and profit-making have spill-over effects that all too often damage human health and landscapes, degrade water and air quality, endanger plant and animal species, and possibly, over time, even alter the very stability of Earth's climate. And the remedy?

Corrective measures will usually require government intervention: first to scientifically verify damages, then to initiate policies—such as a health tax (on cigarettes), a green tax (on emissions), or the trading of pollution credits—and to enforce clean air, water, and endangered species laws or negotiate global agreements (whaling, chlorofluoro-carbons, CO_2, etc.) enforced by protocols, regulatory oversight, and international law.

Conceptually, these measures can be understood in the context of motivating businesses and consumers to pay the *full* direct and indirect costs (full-cost accounting) of their economic activity, including the costs of collateral damages to natural and human environments. Simply put, it's a fairness issue, of playing the "game" (the capitalist game) fair and square. Let us look at a contemporary illustration regarding human health, a concern that was recently brought to my attention by the Physicians for Social Responsibility, an environmental advocacy group in Washington, DC.

Childhood Asthma

The issue is the ever-worsening problem of childhood asthma. Indeed, there's good evidence that asthma is exacerbated by truck and automobile pollution, including elevated ground-level ozone in U.S. cities. Consider the following observations reported by a *U.S. News and World Report* article on the subject of transportation gridlock and urban sprawl:

> During the 1996 Olympics, Atlanta officials took dramatic steps to limit car traffic in the city. The measures worked so well that

the number of cars in the morning rush hour dropped by 22.5 percent. But there was another benefit:

The number of children suffering asthma attacks, a leading cause of childhood illness, dropped dramatically.[1]

Atlanta's inadvertent experiment and its intriguing results dovetail with other studies suggesting that ozone increases the incidence of asthmatic attacks (especially for inner-city children).

Armed with this information, I approached a Wisconsin state lawmaker asking if he would consider initiating a modest increase in our state's gas tax (say, five cents) earmarked not for the usual highway construction and maintenance, but to reimburse parents for asthma-related expenses. I told him that I was upset because I was paying *too little* for my gas, disturbed that I was not paying my fair share of the spillover effects of my driving.

I asked why we should force families with sick children to subsidize an artificially low-cost transportation system. Relevant expenses might include:

- emergency trips to the hospital
- wages lost attending sick children
- asthma medication, inhalers, charcoal-impregnated face masks
- doctor's fees and higher insurance premiums

Drivers, I added, should also be responsible for the extra costs of rescheduling outdoor sporting events, since many asthmatic children are forced to remain indoors during periodic ozone alerts. An increase in our federal and/or state gasoline tax would be a good beginning, a step towards a fair, full-cost accounting.

Any increase in fuel prices, whether through market forces (as in 2008) or a pollution tax, will create hardships, yes, but benefits too, including cleaner air and, as economists predict, fewer traffic deaths and injuries. Also, with higher gas prices, there will be more investments in biking and walking trails. Indeed, walkers and bikers in some cities have already pressured local governments to promote more walkable and bike-friendly neighborhoods. Whereas Atlanta is infamous for its *un*walkability, Portland, Oregon, the other extreme, has some sixteen pedestrian districts where the street design, sidewalks, and traffic laws give pedestrians priority. And in Davis, California, there are safe, dedicated bike lanes on most city streets. Moreover, developers in Davis are required to provide bike access to new residential and commercial developments.

Full-cost accounting would also encourage more carpooling and, if available, greater use of public transit. Not only would urban adults and children breathe easier, but trees and wildlife would too. And finally, if truckers and car owners paid their full direct and indirect costs, economists believe these extra costs would begin to reduce road congestion while diminishing the political pressure to widen roads and highways, thus minimizing damage to local communities and to the landscape itself.

Of course, the economist's perspective—even with good science, logic, and sensible remedies on its side—is usually no match for well-funded special interests. In the case of increasing gas taxes for legitimate spillover costs, the powerful highway, oil, and automobile lobbies will often block legislation that would (as they see it), harm their industries. Indeed, in response to my gas tax suggestion, my representative told me, "I understand your point and yes, I even agree with you," but then added, "Jim, you'd better forget it, politically it ain't going to happen."

Ecologist's Perspective

I dream of a day when parents, children, politicians, economists, CEOs, bankers, miners, and loggers, among others, make decisions based upon a genuine ecological consciousness, including an understanding and full appreciation of the broad spectrum of environmental values that allow ecosystems to be healthy and whole.

As an example, consider the issue of logging in an old-growth forest, such as the few that still exist in the United States. In what ways would the ecologists' perspective differ from that of a for-profit capitalist? To answer this question, I find it helpful to picture in my mind an image of a playground Teeter-Totter that has a large, colorful basket at each end. The basket on the left side represents capitalist values and the one on the right represents ecological values. Children begin placing weighted objects representing the different sets of values in each basket. What weights would they put into the capitalist values basket? Benefits might include:

- the monetary value of wood products (including export earnings), incomes for loggers, truckers, and sawmill operators
- increased sales for equipment, including manufacturing jobs
- an increase in these companies' short-term profits
- corporate stock prices that would go up, adding value to stock-holder portfolios

Importantly, from the for-profit point of view, there would be pressure to maximize these values in the short turn by clear-cutting the forest.

Now turning our attention to the right side (ecological values), what representative weights would the children put into their basket? In some old-growth forests (such as the Menominee Indian Reservation in Wisconsin), tribes engage in logging, which provides modest economic benefits while also maintaining their forest's original ecological makeup for generations. The Menominee remove a relatively small portion of the forest each year using sustainable yield management principles that incorporate selective cutting based on cultural constraints laid down by tribal elders over a hundred years ago. With this selective cutting strategy, there is some monetary value gained from lumber, logging, sawmill operator's jobs, and some export profits. The return in the short run is lower (compared to clear-cutting), yet over many years, income would be relatively stable.

Now in addition to the modest economic benefits, let's ask the children to put into their basket the following weights representing a broader spectrum of ecological, scientific, and spiritual values:

- a habitat for endangered plants and animals
- the possibility of discovering new and effective wonder drugs from the forest's plant life
- a "living classroom" to study a healthy ecosystem
- a source of beauty, inspiration, and spiritual sustenance
- cooler, cleaner, and healthier streams and rivers (compared to a clear-cut forest)
- the recycling of nutrients and the production of new topsoil
- the ability to sequester atmospheric carbon and generate oxygen

Tropical forests may also produce a sustainable supply of nuts, berries, valuable barks, tubers, mushrooms, and medicines for those who know how to find them. From an ecological perspective, forests roll up their sleeves and work hard to provide invisible yet important benefits, or so-called ecological services, based on the productivity of the forests' intrinsic natural capital.

When we compare them, the children's ecological-values basket ought to easily outweigh the capitalist basket. Yet in our current global economic arrangement of ultrapowerful forces of corrupt politics, obsession with unfettered free trade—plus, of course, inflated greed and short-run profit maximization—we find that the capitalist basket usually wins out. It's as if the global economy were defying gravity as well as other vital laws of nature.

The Prairie's Perspective

If I were asked to pick an analogy from which I might learn the principles for a future capitalism, my choice would be a native prairie ecosystem I walk by nearly every day. Some would think my example a little odd; it's not exactly global free-market capitalism, but more a living example of what might be called *local* natural capitalism. Indeed, my prairie has become a mentor for me, as if it were trying to teach its lessons to a slow-learning yet earnest economics student. Nevertheless, I have now discovered that this flowering grassland is not only attractive but exceptionally diverse, and, like a model sustainable economy, remarkably productive, turning sunbeams into biotic beauty and eventually converting vegetation into rich, deep, loamy soils.

In addition, this prairie ecosystem has achieved something quite amazing: an exquisite balance between life and death, humming along year after year in a kind of steady-state, economic efficiency. It recycles virtually everything and unfailingly and blooms anew, spring after spring and every summer too!

Prairies are resilient in severe drought, yet they can also handle a week of drenching rain. Moles, monarch butterflies, and meadowlarks survive there. Blue stems and Indian grasses live in prairies too, and so do black-eyed Susans, purple prairie clovers, stiff goldenrods, and late-summer blooms of blazing stars.

Sometimes I also enjoy simply lying down in the prairie, accepting gravity, as it were, my back stretched out along the rough ground, my eyes taking in sun, cloud, flower, seedpod, and there high above me, tufts of grasses bending down and up, up and down, as if there were an invisible ocean of windblown waves.

So one might ask: What direction, what trajectory will we be able to follow to a more natural, indeed a more balanced capitalism? Can meadowlark values readjust and redress capitalism's spillover effects and correct its corrosive externalities?

Can we conserve (as if an ecological consciousness were our second nature) our planet's grasslands, soils, ancient forests, subterranean waters, its oceans, rivers, and reefs? Like the prairie, can we find a more harmonic, natural equilibrium that abounds in beauty, balance, and biodiversity? And finally, can we utilize renewable energies and make consumables durable (and fully recyclable) while preserving Earth's realms of amazement, its landscapes of surprise?

Chapter 3

A Compensatory Ethic

One of the penalties of an ecological education is that one lives alone in a world of wounds.

—Aldo Leopold

Some fifty years ago, wildlife ecologist Aldo Leopold wove various ideas together into a memorable weave he called "The Land Ethic." To Leopold's credit, the essay has become the centerpiece vision for ecologists, preservationists, and outdoors people alike. Indeed, I've seen no better definition of meadowlark values than can be found in this essay and others from his classic, *A Sand County Almanac.*

In "The Land Ethic," Leopold asserts that we are "members of a community of interdependent parts" and that it is time to consider enlarging the boundaries of that community to include not just humans but plants, animals, soils, lakes, rivers, and oceans, or collectively, the *land.*

Recognition of this broader community carries with it a commitment of coexistence with and protection of all the diverse natural entities. In short, Leopold challenged us to begin rethinking the role of *Homo sapiens* from "conqueror of the land community to plain member or citizen of it."

"Plain member." I especially appreciate that word "plain," a word that implies an uncharacteristic dose of humility. As we move away from the role of land conqueror, many now believe that we must begin to fairly share Earth's finite resources. This, in turn, would imply a profound alteration of our consumption habits and standard of living expectations. In his vision, Leopold has begun to describe one of the ultimate goals of our species: a true transformation toward an ecological consciousness on a worldwide scale. It is a goal that even Leopold realized would take generations to accomplish.

In the meantime what can be done? Are there any intermediate ethical stances we can use as stepping-stones along the way? Let me suggest one: a *compensatory ethic.* Compensate is defined as: "to make up for or to offset; counterbalance; to make equivalent or satisfactory reparation to."

A compensatory ethic would surely be less revolutionary than the land ethic. It would not demand that we radically alter our personal economic lives, nor necessarily shun material abundance around the world. It does, however, imply that if we wish to continue with our resource-using, high-energy, materialistic habits, we should begin to compensate or mitigate the damage by offsetting the negative consequences of our consumption.

An illustration of compensatory ethical action was a decision by an electrical utility—Applied Energy Services of Arlington, Virginia—to help finance the planting of fifty million tress in Guatemala. This investment was a good-faith commitment to compensate for the utility's annual carbon dioxide emissions (or "carbon footprint") by planting future carbon dioxide absorbers. Within the last ten years, other industries have followed suit either by earning "carbon credits" (utilizing efficient, renewable energy sources) or by agreeing to buy up credits so that a business may temporarily continue with inefficient processes.

At the UN Climate Conference held in Bali, Indonesia in 2007, tropical rainforest countries began to move ahead with the following compensatory ethic proposal for industrial nations: if you want our biodiversity and you also want to continue using a disproportionate amount of fossil fuels, you can "rent" our natural CO_2 absorbers. Undisturbed rainforests would take on monetary value as tradable carbon credits that could be bought and sold in a global carbon market.

Another approach would be to impose a CO_2 user tax (or carbon tax) on technologies and products that use fossil fuels. The revenues could be used to subsidize the economic survival of traditional tropical forest populations that might otherwise be endangering plants and animals by their traditional slash-and-burn farming techniques.

If one accepts this line of argument and makes a commitment to explore compensatory ethical options, a number of creative alternatives will become obvious to both consumers and businesses.

A few years ago, for example, I passed by the site of a new big-box retail store. Its enormous parking lot (then empty of cars) looked like a miniature blackened desert. I paced the lot's perimeter and found it to be roughly 134 by 143 steps, or approximately 19,000 square yards, a sizeable area with no soils or animals—not even a weed!

With such a sealing of the land, our compensatory ethic cries out for the company and its car-habituated customers (like myself) to make amends for suffocating the soil and radically altering its environment. Couldn't the corporation arrange to preserve a natural habitat—a rare forest grove, a remnant prairie, or a marshland perhaps? Or how about a contribution to the Nature Conservancy, an organization that has demonstrated an expertise at this kind of thing?

It would be but a modest investment that would help restore some habitat gained for habitat lost. If voluntary contributions were not forthcoming, perhaps a paving fee would be the way to go. Personally, I would feel much better about patronizing such stores if I was assured that they had paid their dues in some way, and were fully committed to a corporate compensatory ethic.

Compensatory ethics is a topic that's challenging to think about and also fun to discuss. There are, for example, certain types of projects and developments that many agree would be simply too destructive to apply the compensatory ethic to: oil development in the Arctic National Wildlife Refuge comes to mind, as does mountaintop removal mining in Appalachia. With global warming threats already underway worldwide, perhaps it's time to stop building (and eventually shut down) *all* coal-fired power plants unless companies learn how to prevent additional greenhouse gas emissions by sequestering the carbon dioxide produced when coal is burned. On the global level, it would be desirable, perhaps essential, not only to stabilize CO_2 levels (currently at 385–390 parts per million) but to develop lifestyles and technologies to actually *reduce* CO_2 levels to a safer long-term level of 350 parts per million.[1]

On the individual level, creativity plus a little ecological understanding is all that's needed to spin out a variety of strategies. Consider, for example, the ecological implications of deciding to have a child. How might one apply compensatory ethics to such a decision?

In my writing study I use both photovoltaic and passive solar panels for electricity, but I also burn wood. Recently I vowed to plant or preserve as many trees as I burn each year. This ethic is just common sense and not much of a burden. I'm surprised how blind I've been to such a meadowlark value in thirty years of burning wood. Furthermore, I will compensate in other ways as well. Eventually I'm aiming to adopt a simpler, less consumptive lifestyle, thereby reducing my compensatory debt.

So, all you readers, consumers, and businesspeople alike—what are your compensatory commitments? If we can make headway with this and other ethical stepping-stones (wending our way toward Leopold's land ethic), then our home planet Earth—so pained and pummeled over the years—might spin with relief, knowing we were doing our best to restore and preserve her astonishing aliveness, diversity, and ever-surprising beauty.

Chapter 4

Craftsmanship and Salvation

After a long time, I felt that I had to choose one way of living or the other.... I took heart again in the old ways and did what my father had told me to do, carve [stone] monuments to my people, small monuments. And then my life changed. A new spirit came back into me and my life became so great that the sky could not contain it and the wind and rivers could not move it.

—Gerard Rancourt Tsonakwa

For some years now, I have had an argument with my father. He believes that we all move forward by enlarging our individual and collective productivity. He tells me that we must grow "two blades of grass where only one grew before." Efficiency and productivity, he says, have not only given us our present standard of living but will also be the driving forces for a better future. What are the tools that will bring this about? "More investment and improved technology" is his answer.

I have always felt that though his position was generally correct, there was something important missing, but I was never quite able to put my finger on it. After all, isn't driving more efficient than biking or walking? And why do I use a gas-engine lawn mower rather than the old-fashioned human powered one? My intuition went awry when I objectively observed my own behavior.

But now I believe I know what has been troubling me all these years. It is simply this: modern machinery, technology, and the "cult of efficiency" destroys our age-old cultural need to periodically engage in slow-paced, traditional craftsmanship.

Now when I speak of a lack of craftsmanship, I am not referring to the common complaint today that many of our products are shoddy and poorly designed, though to some degree this is true. Craftsmanship involves more than that. To me, craftsmanship implies a particular *attitude* toward the shaping of raw materials, while the final product is often secondary.

Though outwardly inefficient, inwardly a craftsperson gains a sense of deep satisfaction, even reverence, for raw materials and tools skillfully used. For American and British writers among others, the raw material is the richness of words themselves within the universe of the English language. (W. H. Auden once wrote that if a person came to him and said, "I have important things to say," he or she would not likely become a poet. But if they said, "I feel like hanging around words, listening to what they say,"[1] then Auden felt that this person had a chance.)

The craftworker in glass savors glass, stonecarvers their stone, the furniture craftsman loves his wood. It's much like a love affair in which the craftsperson ultimately gives birth to some fine work or artifact. Sometimes the process is sensuous and, at other times, the worker becomes so totally absorbed that the "self" is forgotten for a moment. It is perhaps something like a child intensively concentrating on play; at other times it may be more like a spiritual experience.

Indeed, most craftsmen whom I have known feel that there is a "sanctuary" quality to their work. Years ago, Minnesota author Robert Pirsig described so beautifully the process of tuning up a motorcycle: "The first tappet is right on, no adjustment required, so I move on to the next ... I always feel like I'm in church when I do this ... The gauge is some kind of religious icon and I'm performing a holy rite with it."[2]

Elsewhere in his book *Zen and the Art of Motorcycle Maintenance,* Pirsig demonstrates that motorcycle maintenance can be an art that leads to an in-the-present experience akin to Zen, where the pain of the past and the anxieties of the future are dissolved as the worker becomes one with the work.

Now consider your friends and relatives. How many true craft-workers do you know? Why are there so few? And why hasn't modern technology—especially the widespread use of labor-saving devices—given us that broad margin of leisure time to pursue quality crafts? Though I certainly don't know all the reasons, I do know that when we make an obsession out of efficiency and high-speed technologies, we are more likely to diminish our respect for any process that appears to be "inefficient." Furthermore, our high standard of living has given us so many choices that we feel compelled to experience or consume as many possibilities as are within our reach, thus "efficient use of time" is the order of the day.

And yet, deep down, I suspect that many of us regret the loss of crafts-manship. I feel confident in saying this because I observe that people respond with genuine awe when they see a piece of fine work from the hands of a true craftsperson, such as handmade furniture, blown glass, a beautiful quilt, or a well-crafted poem. We read with envy and respect about the craftspeople of Appalachia, preservers of blacksmithing, herbal gathering, stone masonry, and the making of musical instruments, just to name a few. We know that somewhere, sometime we too would like to return to this world of relaxed pace, of deliberateness, and of carefully (slowly!) creating artifacts that reflect what Pirsig called "Quality."

Perhaps what we are really seeking is a kind of salvation. Some readers may recall that in the final chapter of his classic, *Walden,* Henry David Thoreau suggests that the true craftsman will never die. Our technocrats and ministers of efficiency would do well to remember the account of the Kouroo artist who strove for perfection in the carving of a walking staff: After many years of working on it—with endless love, patience and complete absorption, he found that "his singleness of purpose and resolution ... endowed him ... with perennial youth." His friends died, dynasties came and went, and even the polestar changed its position! Then at last, when he finally completed his task, the staff "suddenly expanded before the eyes of the astonished artist into the fairest of all creations of Brahma."

> He had made a new system in making a staff, a world with full and fair proportions in which, though the old cities and dynasties had passed away and fairer and more glorious ones had taken their places, the material was pure, and his art was pure. How could the result be other than wonderful?[3]

Chapter 5

An Ideal Boss

Where other companies speak of a supervisor or foreman, IBM speaks of an assistant ... He is to be the "assistant" to his workers. His job is to be sure that they know their work and have tools. He is not their boss.

—Peter Drucker

As we explore meadowlark values, we might want to take a moment to consider the ecology of the workplace, especially the all-important worker/supervisor relationship. If you are like me, you've probably thought about the question, "What are the qualifications for an ideal boss?" This individual might be a supervisor in a business, the armed forces, or perhaps in a university or government agency. Since "supervisor" and "boss" have connotations which do not always fit the ideal, let's use instead the softer term *administrator,* a designation less hierarchical, more plastic, and therefore more open to creative interpretation than the conventional terms.

What then should our model administrator do or not do? What are his or her functions within the organization, and how does this person differ from the traditional "bosses" of today? Undoubtedly every business writer has his or her own list of skills and competencies needed to become the so-called "effective manager." For my ideal administrator, however, let me suggest four characteristics.

Gardener

I use this term because gardeners, especially organic gardeners, see their present activity in terms of the long run. Like characters in an ancient Chinese fable, they look for a payoff far into the future. Good gardeners, for example, prepare their soil for years ahead. Aware of long-term nutrient cycles, these gardeners begin gathering materials in the form of old hay, kitchen scraps, and manure to make compost that may not break down for a year or two. Once the compost is added to the soil, the gardener will not see results until much later. With this kind of time perspective, gardeners tend to be optimists in the sense that they are convinced that small decisions today will add considerable quality to the enterprise many years hence.

In addition, gardeners seem to enjoy the art of experimenting, and they don't get too upset if projects sometimes fail. They're anxious to try new varieties, different ways of planting, and novel ways to build up topsoil—things that add interest and excitement and offer the experimenter something to look forward to.

The administrator-as-gardener views his or her operating unit in a similar way, with the goal being the long-term success of the enterprise and the well-being of the workers. The administrator should offer encouragement, praise, and opportunities for individual development, knowing that these actions may not have a payoff immediately but will surely nurture happier, more loyal, and more productive workers for the long run.

Using the gardener as a model, the administrator should also encourage experimentation and expect some failure, for this is what makes the job interesting and creates possibilities for true innovation. This role is the administrator's most satisfying, for it offers the greatest potential for making lasting improvements.

Intervener

Of all the characteristics, this one comes closest to the conventional "boss." The head of a unit must communicate the larger objectives or mission of the organization to the workers. Combined with this duty, he or she has the responsibility to intervene in those cases in which a worker disregards the goals as defined by the hierarchy. Judgments must be made quickly when such behavior seems likely to threaten the reputation or effectiveness of the unit. Nothing is more demoralizing to the rank-and-file staff than when the unit's reputation wanes and others begin to view the worker's group with diminishing esteem, particularly when the problem lies with just one or two individuals. Such a problem can often be brought to a halt by one's coworkers, but when they fail, the administrator must intervene or the end result may well be more control and regimentation imposed by the hierarchy.

This kind of intervention involves an immense amount of tact, plus an ability to criticize and persuade the individual to change his or her actions without permanently damaging the worker's sense of self-worth. If the one-to-one intervention does not work, then the administrator must sound out the staff for their suggestions for handling the situation. In extreme cases, psychological help may be in order. As a last resort, there may be no choice but to fire the worker. Whatever the solution, the administrator must know how to handle this delicate situation with skill and diplomacy. It is, as we all know, not an easy job.

Resource Person

The third function of our ideal administrator is that of resource person. Many supervisors find this skill the most difficult to learn. For a good model, let me suggest a once-common role in the health care industry: a hospital administrator's relationship to the doctors.

In these settings, the administrator is not the boss, but more a *servant*. The administrator regards the doctors as professionals who know best how to do what they are doing. The administrator is hired to take care of details such as patients' records, equipment purchasing, and marketing. A good administrator in this role ought to be visiting various departments asking questions such as "What can I do for you?" or "How might I make your job easier?" Although this approach may sound logical, how often do we hear such kind and helpful words from our supervisors?

The main thing to keep in mind is that administrators should *always regard their employees as experts in their respective fields* who, from time to time, will need extra services or resources that only someone in an administrative position can provide. I see no reason why this attitude cannot be applied in the executive suites of General Motors, in the administration of a university, an army, or government department, or even between worker and foreman on an assembly line.

Lobbyist

In all large organizations, you will find competition between departments and divisions for scarce resources. These resources are usually thought of in terms of money and staffing. But they might also include other benefits such as the quality of the workplace, access to policy-making, flexibility, and other tangibles and intangibles that are conferred by the hierarchy.

Therefore an administrator should learn a little of the art of politics and public relations. There will be times when the lobbyist role demands even more than the usual political representation, especially when the survival of the unit is in question. On such occasions, an administrator must know how to negotiate effectively, to defend with skill and determination the vital interests of the department. He or she must know how to deal with subtle power plays of others who may be out to destroy. In such times, good administrators must convince the hierarchy that their workers are not only making short-term contributions to the larger organization, but are working hard toward the long-term objectives as well.

Of course, this kind of political activity can be an especially unpleasant business. Administrators may feel it necessary to make friends with people they do not particularly like. They may sometimes have to advertise the unit's virtues or minimize certain faults.

Unfortunately, many individuals in this role feel the need to overlook illegalities such as misrepresentation of balance sheets or other financial weaknesses (as happened in the case of certain Wall Street firms in 2007 and 2008), or engaged in bribes, or kickbacks; they might lie about ineffective or dangerous products; or (in violation of meadowlark values), poison the environment. Such unethical actions will often catch up with the person in question—first on a personal, moral basis, then with the organization, and finally, publicly. When this happens, they jeopardize the morale and possibly the survival of the department or, at the very least, destroy the progress that had taken years to build up as a resource person and gardener. When an administrator engages in such questionable activities, it is essential that the people within the unit act as the intervener; at first privately, then publicly if necessary.

Nevertheless, the ideal administrator must be realistic about power relationships within the organization and at times defend the unit against dangerous encroachments that can and do take place in any political arena.

Still, if the lobbyist function is performed well, there can be no better payoff than to have the staff respect their ideal boss; respect, in turn, makes their roles that much easier in nurturing the unit's health, growth, and well-being of all concerned.

Chapter 6

A Passion for Learning

Years ago, I wrote that many people in their worst nightmares find themselves once again a student in school.... Many mature and competent adults tell me that to this day they feel uneasy in a school building, as if they were guilty of some crime, but didn't know what.

—John Holt

Is it, I wonder, possible to teach meadowlark values? Of course some teachers make an effort to encourage students to know about geology and geography as well as about local plants, animals, and their intricate ecological relationships. Others teach about climate change, green energy, and sustainable economic development.

Yet I wonder if teachers should aim for something more, something beyond knowledge itself. What is it?

The goal of teaching, in my view, is to somehow instill a *passion for learning.* If teachers are doing their job, they will help their students acquire a lifetime love of learning. The objective is not the result of short-term scores on standardized tests, but the long-run delight of continuous learning and deepening understanding until the end of their lives. If teachers don't somehow move their students toward this objective, even in a small way, I don't think they can be considered completely successful.

Deep down, I have a feeling that nurturing a passion for learning should not be difficult. The process of growing and becoming a more self-reliant learner, of prospecting for humankind's creations and discoveries, ought to be an exciting adventure full of delights and surprises that touch both heart and mind.

Yet as we all know, this is often not the case. Teachers with enthusiasm and the best of intentions frequently end up as mechanical dispensers of information and facts. Many feel that the only way they can overcome the students' resistance to learning is to "force-feed" them by methods of power and fear.

Power and fear! These seem to be the tools used to get the job done. What a frustrating environment this must be for a new teacher with high hopes and good intentions. And from the viewpoint of the students who recall the fun of learning new things on their own before schooling, and who wish to become persons of greater value later on in their lives, the situation is even worse. Such students must feel robbed. What was once an inner-directed drive for learning is now based upon trying to please the teacher or worse, pass the mandated tests, so that one can successfully "get through the system." For those who eventually want to become self-learners, undoing the damage is very difficult, if not impossible, like trying to decontaminate radioactive substances.

Is there any hope for this unfortunate state of affairs? Under our current schooling system the prospects appear dim, yet it is interesting to note the few cases in which these suffocating habits and attitudes did not occur. For example, among the various teachers I have known, a few have been able to avoid these pitfalls. They did not succumb to the usual mechanical teaching. Instead, they retained their enthusiasm year after year, and what is even more amazing, they succeeded in nurturing a genuine excitement for learning—surely a meadowlark value if there ever was one. But what was their secret? What qualities did these memorable teachers have in common?

From my observations, each possessed three characteristics. First, these teachers put a high priority on creating a positive attitude toward their subject matter, as opposed to the usual goal of simply imparting a certain body of knowledge. It's not that knowledge and facts were unimportant, but the information is used more as a vehicle to get students excited about the process of learning. Teachers can tell if they are on the right track by listening to their students. Such comments as: "Boy, do I love economics!" or "I think I will audit history class from her" demonstrate a healthy attitude, one that is a good indicator that self-learning is not far off.

The second ability is to knit together other areas of knowledge into the teacher's own discipline, and also into the student's experiences and current level of knowledge. This quality implies that the teacher herself is interested in diverse subjects and thus is a good model for self-learning.

I believe students often feel a certain disconnectedness as they travel from one box of knowledge to another. The sum often becomes less than the disconnected parts. Unfortunately students rarely develop the skills that will help them tie these seemingly disconnected parts together.

When a holistic integration is done expertly such as with a Carl Sagan, Loren Eiseley, or Lewis Thomas, the performance can be breathtaking. Yet there seems to be little or no attempt in our schools, from kindergarten to graduate school, to cultivate these integrative skills or reward teachers who pursue them. Perhaps it is collegial pressures or simply ingrained teaching habits that make it so difficult for teachers to climb over the high walls of discipline specialization as we pursue our day-to-day dealings with students.

But now let us assume that we can avoid the problems cited above. Also assume that we are able to retain our enthusiasm—and yet, we still find our students unhappy and resentful. It's a situation in which things ought to be OK, but instead we find resistance to change and growth;

we simply have not awakened in our students their innate potential for learning. What's wrong? What have we missed?

This brings us to the third and perhaps most difficult quality, for it involves some decontamination on the part of the teachers themselves. The third quality that good teachers have is a high regard for the student. Actually, it's more than that. These teachers consistently demonstrate a profound *respect* for their students' native intelligence and their potential for discovery.

This means, for example, that teachers of physics would give the same respect, the same esteem, to each individual student that they would to the great geniuses of the discipline; for example to a young Marie Curie or to an Albert Einstein if they were sitting in the classroom.

For many teachers, this third quality involves a radical rethinking of what education is all about. Indeed, we find no simple techniques that will help teachers out on this one. But when respect is there, it is there. The students know it. Respect is transmitted in a thousand little ways, operating like a magic whirlpool that loosens up tight muscles of resistance and thaws out cold fear.

When teachers truly respect their students, the relationship is no longer one based on power, but on equality. When a student says something impressive, the teacher is truly impressed and, indeed, might learn something new as well. The essential source of authority teachers have is some extra knowledge in an interesting or useful discipline—nothing more. Traditional authority and power have no place in the relationship.

In the end, respect brings respect, resulting in a situation in which students may actually become engaged learners, often in surprising ways. Those few successful teachers know the truth of this. How did they learn it? Perhaps by trial and error, perhaps by instinct—I don't know. I wish I did.

However, I do know that teachers who combine these three qualities—a positive attitude, integrated presentations, and a deep respect for their students—will, in their own small way, move their students closer to becoming self-reliant and sensitive learners. These students may now begin to develop a healthy set of values, to evolve a personal philosophy while gaining sufficient confidence to adapt to life's ever-changing problems. All these are the fruits of teachers passing on one of the great goals of a lifetime—a passion for learning.

Chapter 7

Topsoil Drama

The care of the earth is our most ancient and most worthy and, after all, our most pleasing responsibility. To cherish what remains of it, and to foster its renewal, is our only legitimate hope.

—Wendell Berry

Topsoil, we know, makes life possible on this planet. Yet how many of us realize that creating topsoil is a slow, slow process and losing it can be dishearteningly swift? Surely these are important facts for all of us to know, and especially important to impress upon young people.

With this thought in mind, I felt that a natural history of soils might be a useful, even fun topic when my wife asked me to do a project for her Girl Scout day camp. Starting with a suggestion from Del Thomas, a local soil scientist, we therefore decided to create a "topsoil drama." In addition, we tried to make our little play relatively simple so that others might try it with a minimum of cost and preparation. Here then is an account of what we did:

We gathered the twenty girls, aged seven to twelve, for a one-hour activity. I began by suggesting they pick up some topsoil and asked, "How important is this in keeping you alive?" The question created an opportunity for all of us to think through the essential nature of what we negatively refer to as "dirt." Of course, all our vegetables, our fruit, and our grains are directly dependent upon soil, and most everything else we eat is indirectly dependent upon it as well.

How about a pizza? How do the ingredients, including the meat, directly or indirectly depend upon topsoil? What about lumber for our homes, paper for books and writing, cotton and wool to keep us warm? What about butterflies and bumblebees, foxes and meadowlarks? Yes, all of us depend upon a food chain that begins with the miracle of water, sunlight, and seeds, combined with this dark crumbly substance ever present beneath our feet.

Next question: "Where does soil come from?" Here I brought out a jar of water with a tablespoon of alum mixed in. (The alum, which can be purchased at a grocery store, helps separate the various soil components.)

We then put a handful of our collected soil into the water, screwed the lid tight and let everyone give the jar a shake. Within a minute it became obvious that our soil had at least three components: first, the small stones and sand that remained on the bottom; next, the silty or fine clay particles of the middle, and finally, the decomposed vegetable matter floating on top. After observing this, I asked the girls if they would like to be in a play in which we could "make" some soil.

"Yes!" they shouted unanimously.

"OK, let's begin at the beginning—that is, with rock from an ancient volcano, which over time is broken up by wind and water. Which of you wants to be a volcano?" Many hands shot up. I chose a volunteer and placed a prepared VOLCANO sign around her neck. From our son's rock collection I had brought along a sample of volcanic rock in the form of a hand-sized piece of lightweight pumice. We passed it around and then gave it back to the girl designated Volcano.

"Anyone want to be Water?" I got a couple of volunteers and gave them WATER signs. "Now who wants to be Wind?"

I explained that wind and water "will act on these rocks as they did over billions of years, to break up the volcanic rock into smaller and smaller pieces of sand and stone." I also pointed out that these sand particles were moved about by water and eventually came to rest. There they sat. And with more and more sand coming in, compressing the bottom, the layers became tightly packed together, as if they were cemented together.

This newer, compressed rock we called bedrock sandstone. (In our area, we have many outcroppings of Cambrian sandstones dating back about five hundred million years.) I pulled out a piece of local sandstone and asked, "Who wants to play the part of Bedrock?" I chose six or seven Bedrocks, put signs on them, and asked these girls to huddle together on the ground. Now when we start our topsoil drama, Wind and Water will "wave" and "blow" through Bedrock, breaking it back into individual, unglued sand particles.

Next, I asked someone to be Glacier. (Here in the Midwest, glaciers came through at various times in the past two million years, ripping up bedrock, grinding the pieces down, and carrying the soil-making material to our area. Some of the sand in our jar, I pointed out, may have come from hundreds of miles north.) Glacier, in our little drama, had the job of "crunching and grinding" and moving bedrock sand particles across the landscape.

The rest of the girls, except one, were given signs representing small to microscopic animals (including moles, worms, mites, insect larvae, nematodes, and bacteria) and still others would be plants. As plants, they would fall on the ground, wriggle up, fall down, wriggle up, again and again in imitation of the endless cycle of plants growing, dying, and growing again.

At this point, we briefly returned to the jar of water and soil. I showed the Plant girls that they would become the floating humus (decayed matter) on top, while the finer particles would be in the middle, and the broken up bedrock would end up as sand at the bottom of the jar.

Finally, the one remaining girl played Mother Time. Her job was to hold her hands up and hover over all the topsoil drama activity.

The play could now begin. And what a scene it was! Volcano's pumice was thrown up again and again. Wind and Water broke up Bedrock while Glacier bumped about and moved the Bedrock even more. Meanwhile, Plants grew up, died, and grew up and died again, at a steady pace as Animals did their important work. After a few minutes, I asked them to stop while taking a moment to appreciate how much time must pass to make soil.

"Once bedrock is broken up, it takes approximately five hundred years to make *one inch* of topsoil!"

"Let's now pretend that ten seconds is a hundred years of time," I said. "Everyone freeze and consider all the things that are happening. Mother Time will hold her hands over the scene, and we will call out every one hundred years (every ten seconds). Remember, nobody can move. You must simply think about everything going on."

"One hundred years … two hundred years … three hundred years …" Frozen kids. Each ten seconds seemed unbearably long. "Four hundred years … and finally five hundred years.

"And after all this work, here is what we have." I pulled a towel off a pie pan and on the bottom was one inch of soil. It was a grand achievement!

"But," I asked, "is it enough to grow a tree?"

"No."

"Could it grow a stalk of corn?"

"No."

A small seedling, at best, might grow in our inch of soil. We would obviously have to make many, many inches to grow a tree.

While we were discussing this last point, a gust of wind came through, creating an opportunity to demonstrate wind erosion. Picking up some soil from the pan, I let it blow out of my hands. Another handful, and most of the soil was gone. I was now beginning to sense an element of frustration, even anger: all that work! All that time put into making our inch of topsoil, and now it was so easily, so quickly lost to the wind. We looked down at the pan. It was a depressing sight—a little bit of soil but mostly spots of bare, polished aluminum. Now we couldn't even grow a seedling.

We then walked over to a worn path that went down a bank to the creek. The trail was bare of vegetation and had begun to show signs of erosion. "Why is the path losing its soil?"

We noted that the vegetation, which contributes to the making of soil, is also important in keeping the soil from washing away, especially on a slope like this. I then put the last of our homemade topsoil on the path and asked the girls where they thought it would eventually end up.

Obviously the next rain would carry our loose soil down to the creek below. We mentally followed its inevitable trip into our local Red Cedar River, to the Chippewa River and the Mississippi, and finally into the Gulf of Mexico. (Here it would have been helpful to have brought along a map of the U.S.) Then, all of us standing still, I once again asked them to remain quiet for a moment and to think about what we had all learned from our little drama.

The long geological and biological processes of soil-building plus the depressing feeling of losing soil to erosion; these were the things I wanted the girls to know, and especially to *feel*. From this experience, they will, hopefully, become more respectful and more vigilant in preserving the wonderful soil we still have—a resource so amazing, so precious, and as we witnessed this day, so very vulnerable, too.

Chapter 8

High Jumping

Of all the formulations of play, the briefest and the best is to be found in Plato's Laws. He sees the model of true playfulness in the need of all young creatures, animal and human, to leap. To truly leap you must learn how to use the ground as a springboard, and how to land resiliently and safely. It means to test the leeway allowed by given limits; to outdo and yet not escape gravity.

—Erik Erickson

Meadowlark values are about healthy bodies as well as healthy learning environments. Doesn't the animal within whisper to us to get up and away from the dull glare of our electronic screens, our pixeled universe, to flee from our seatbound offices and commuter confinements, to *move*, to delight (like all critters) in multifarious motions, activities, and sundry skills?

Consider our urge to run, to launch or hit a ball, to dance away the night, or to execute a karate *smack* (or glide gently into t'ai chi's Wave Hands Like Clouds)—or simply to leap, to *spring up* and test our body's many powers. Most of us have a favorite activity and a story to share; for me, I feel lucky that my athletic urge connects with family culture and early education. It's an odd story that begins over a hundred years ago in the little town of Blue Mound, Illinois.

Family rumor has it that somewhere there's a photo of my grandfather as a young boy, high jumping in the backyard of his Blue Mound home. Someday I'd like to see this picture, for it connects him with me. You see, I love to high jump, too.

In fact, jumping has been a minor passion of mine from grade school right into middle age. Just about everywhere I have ever lived, I have constructed a set of crude high-jump standards and a suitable crossbar. That's pretty much all one needs, that and a soft place to land.

I must confess right off that, despite my obsession with jumping, I'm not a very good jumper. High-schoolers today who jump only as high as I do would not make the track and field team. Years ago, my young son asked me quite honestly if I was "approaching the world's record." (He likes to be proud of his dad, if for no reason other than to brag to his friends.) He soon learned the truth, as verified by his own copy of *The Guinness Book of World Records,* that his father jumps more than three feet below what the best jumpers do. Not very impressive. If my memory is correct, I actually jumped higher in the ninth or tenth grade; but even then, I never made the team.

I'm often haunted by the thought that if I had made the team or had been forced to jump in a phys-ed class, I'd probably now have little, if any, interest in high jumping. I am intrigued, for example, by the late George Sheehan's question, "What happened to our play on our way to becoming adults?" His answer was the following:

> Downgraded by the intellectuals, dismissed by the economists, put aside by the psychologists, it was left to the teachers to deliver the coup de grace. Physical education was born and turned what was joy into boredom, what was fun into drudgery, what was pleasure into work.[1]

One might speculate what other amateur enjoyments and later-life pleasures were also ruined by schooling.

It is therefore not for achievement, honor, or record heights that I jump. I jump simply because I enjoy it. First, I enjoy thinking about the jump beforehand, then translating thought into action—slowly running toward the bar, speeding up on the last step or two, and in a flash, hurtling myself over.

Sometimes I experiment with different speeds, different steps, different zones of concentration. Like any other sport, high jumping can be infinitely complicated or wonderfully simple. The pure analytical side is interesting; but more fun is the sense of abandon, of letting go. Of course, I have yet to feel anything grandiose. For me, there's been no Zen *satori,* no ecstasies to report back. Yet I can honestly say that, once or twice, I've actually felt like I was, well, *flying* (if only for an instant). It was not unlike that wonderful sensation I once felt, when young, in dreams. I've also been able to jump without thinking of anything in particular—just feeling fully connected to my surroundings and to the present moment—feet against dirt, wind and sun on my back, listening to the intermittent sounds of crows and crickets (great jumpers themselves!), and off in the distance, the call of a mourning dove. All the while I am loping toward the bar when suddenly I spring up—converting horizontal momentum into vertical flight.

To jump any reasonable height takes balance, rhythm, coordination, and good form. My jumping style is the old-fashioned Western Roll, first perfected by Stanford high-jumper George Horne in 1912. It is a technique that takes more time to learn than the easy Scissors or the simple Straddle (jumping as if you had tried to leap onto a horse's back and wound up on the other side), or even today's more popular backward leap called "the Fosbury Flop."

In jumping the Western Roll, you take off from your inside foot while kicking your outside foot as hard and as high as you can. As your kicking leg approaches the bar, your body and takeoff leg quickly rise to join the upper leg so that everything "rolls" over pretty much at the same time.

A photograph taken at the instant of clearance shows the jumper as if lying on his side, parallel to the bar, with the kicking leg stretched out and the takeoff leg slightly tucked in near the bar. Unlike some of the other styles, such as the Scissors or Straddle, here everything goes over the bar simultaneously, thus enhancing the sensation of flying.

I was surprised to learn that no recent athlete has broken the world's high-jump record using this technique. But in 1912, Horne cleared six feet, seven inches (a record for his era), and more recently, Gene Johnson cleared a little over seven feet using the Western Roll technique. However, today's best jumpers, using the Fosbury Flop, are currently jumping at or near eight feet!

Let me repeat that I jump because I like to jump. I've jumped in the rain, and I've jumped when there was snow on the ground. Sometimes I'll jump when I don't feel very well. Often I've discovered that the way I jump tells me something about my physical or mental state. I've also discovered that high jumping can be an interesting exercise in learning to confront fear. Anytime you jump at chest level or above, you're taking some physical risk. There the metal bar sits—unwavering, inelastic, and uncompromisingly hard. The bar I currently use is triangular, made of an aluminum alloy, and has sharp edges. If my knee hits it, it can be quite painful. I've also sprained my jumping foot, and it is not unusual for me to hurt my back or wrist.

A good jump puts you relatively high into the air and, sooner or later, you must return to the earth. Yet I've discovered that it's nearly impossible to make a satisfying jump when I have even the slightest air of caution about me. At the moment of takeoff, I must surrender to an instantaneous intuition. A good jump, in short, involves a faith that everything will go perfectly, yet as often happens, a speck of fear intrudes at the last moment, forcing me either to abort or make a miserable and often painful jump. (Could this be a metaphor for other adventures in life?)

So perhaps now you understand why I keep jumping. It's somehow wrapped up in the thrill of animal power, the skill of form, the lighthearted letting go and, sometimes, the feeling of flight. Someday it might be more than that.

Why couldn't high jumping (or any other similar sport) evolve into a more mystical state, such as can be found in the martial arts of Asia? Why couldn't we experience, after sufficient skill development and concentration, something equivalent to what archer Eugen Herrigel describes in his book *Zen in the Art of Archery* as a state of "… serene pulsation which can be heightened into the feeling, otherwise experienced only in rare dreams, of extraordinary lightness, and in the rapturous certainty of being able to summon up energies in any direction."[2]

It's surely something to look forward to. But in the meantime, for me at least, I'll continue my unspectacular leaps. With friendly crickets nearby or thoughts of childhood and Grandpa Bauer jumping in Blue Mound; with corn rustling in the garden, prairie nearby, grass bending in the wind, the sun disappearing behind a cloud, I'm off.

PART II

Henry Thoreau
and Charles Darwin

Chapter 9

Simplify, Simplify: Henry Thoreau as Economic Prophet

So we saunter toward the Holy Land, till one day the sun shall shine more brightly than ever he has done, shall perchance shine into our minds and hearts, and light up our whole lives with a great awakening light, as warm and serene and golden as on a bankside in autumn.

—Henry Thoreau

Henry David Thoreau, the nineteenth-century writer and naturalist, was clearly a pioneer of meadowlark values in the field of economics. Indeed, as a professional economist, I have become more and more convinced that this nineteenth-century American writer was truly a prophet for our time, worthy of the ranks of the major economic philosophers such as Adam Smith, David Hume, Thomas Malthus, and David Ricardo. Let's take a moment to explore some of Thoreau's ideas a little more closely.

Consider, for example, the severe housing crisis of 2008, in which many American families found themselves dangerously overextended, having acquired too much house and taken on too much debt. Many of these families are now stuck with their property, often unable to sell, or are threatened by foreclosure, or have have lost their homes already. Though Thoreau did not specifically predict this particular problem (in his era, it was the overextended farmer that concerned him most), he did make an observation that now seems eerily prophetic. Thoreau warned of the problem of *overabundance* and that our possessions can, at times, "be more easily acquired than got rid of." Change the description slightly—from "barn" to "home"—in the following passage from *Walden* and see how Thoreau's memorable image has a surprisingly contemporary ring to it: "How many a poor immortal soul have I met well-nigh crushed and smothered under its load, creeping down the road of life, pushing before it a barn seventy-five feet by forty, its Augean stables never cleansed … "[1] Thoreau had sympathy for all of us who have too much, whose overabundance turns out to be more of a problem than a solution.

But if material possessions do not represent "the good life," what does? Might it come from the advance of technological conveniences? No doubt Thoreau marveled at and benefitted from many of the by-products of the industrial revolution. He admitted to the advantages of shingles, boards, bricks, and especially glass windowpanes ("doorways of light … like solidified air!"[2]) in the construction of homes. Later in his life Thoreau purchased a small telescope to better see the birds. Also, as a part-time surveyor and pencil maker, he undoubtedly valued the various tools of these different professions. But for the most part, Thoreau felt that inventions tended to be nothing more than "improved means to an unimproved end"[3] or "pretty toys which distract our attention from serious things."[4]

At worst, a particular technology could be greatly destructive. Consider, for example, the famous quote from *Walden,* "… but though a crowd rushes to the depot, and the conductor shouts 'All Aboard!' when the smoke is blown away, and the vapor condensed, it will be perceived that a few are riding, but the rest are run over."[5] Who cannot recognize the chilling prophesy when we consider the death and destruction that's possible with high-tech warfare, a catastrophic leak at a chemical factory, or a nuclear power plant meltdown?

Or consider the giant machines that are used to devour hundreds of square miles of landscape in their pursuit of minerals and trees, or perhaps to reshape acres of farmland for roads, suburban developments, or mile upon mile of big-box stores and shopping malls. "But lo!" Thoreau exclaims, "men have become the tools of their tools." This kind of economic "progress" that ravages the environment would have been especially distressing to Thoreau as he believed that there simply could not be a "good life," nor even a completely healthy life, without access to nature. He once wrote, "There can be no very black melancholy to him who lives in the midst of nature and has his senses still."[6]

In foreshadowing the relatively new discipline of environmental psychology by a century or more, Thoreau prescribed the health benefits of literally immersing oneself in nature:

> We need the tonic of wildness—to wade sometimes in marshes where the bittern and the meadow-hen lurk, and hear the booming of the snipe; to smell the whispering sedge where only some wilder and more solitary fowl builds her nest, and the mink crawls with its belly close to the ground.[7]

Picture now this young man of thirty-four, standing before the Concord Lyceum in the spring of 1851 and opening his lecture with: "I wish to speak a word for Nature, for absolute freedom and wildness," and ending with the oft-quoted, "In wilderness is the preservation of the world."[8]

His audience must have found these ideas very strange since there was an immense area of pure wilderness still existing on the North American continent at that time. Today it is not difficult for us to understand that Thoreau's passion for wilderness values and the preservation of wild spaces was indeed a truly prophetic idea.

Thoreau wished that we might value our natural environment and work hard to preserve it against inevitable encroachments. But what else did he advocate? What would he recommend for individuals to improve their private lives? His answer was as profound as it was brief: "Simplify, simplify!"[9] To exaggerate his point, he advised his readers to "keep your accounts on your thumbnail."[10] More realistically, Thoreau advocated that we reduce our economic needs; that is, engage in a kind of *"voluntary poverty"*[11] (or as some say, *comfortable frugality*). His greatest skill, he once remarked, has been "to want but little."[12] Another prophetic notion? Perhaps so, especially when we consider that, sooner or later, those of us in the rich countries will be forced into lifestyles requiring less use of energy and natural resources.

If Thoreau were alive today he would be appalled by our tremendous private and public debt, our growing dependence on government, and the myriad of specialists who reduce our capacity for doing things for ourselves. He would be also be advocating greater local economic production, as much as was practical. He once suggested that we might learn to grow our own food as well as build our own homes. For recreation, instead of costly prepackaged commercial experiences (shopping, watching a movie, visiting Disneyland, etc.), Thoreau would suggest we simply take a walk in the spirit of adventure or of pilgrimage—"of sauntering toward the Holy Land" as he described it in his essay, "Walking." Thoreau would not only be entertained and educated by his sauntering excursions, but would often gain experiences and observations for his future books and essays.

If in these and other ways we could advance toward the simpler lifestyle that our Concord economist suggests, wouldn't our feelings of economic inadequacy lose some of their sting, the threat of inflation lose some of its terror? Wouldn't our feverish anxiety over economic growth diminish? And, in general, wouldn't life itself be more pleasant if we could slow down and become a little less serious in our striving for high material comfort? Thoreau honestly felt that, with some modest readjustment in our expectations, we might view human existence in a more positive light: "In short, I am convinced, both by faith and experience, that to maintain one's self on this earth is not a hardship but a pastime, if we will live simply and wisely ... "[13]

Thoreau, as economic prophet, asks us to reexamine our basic economic premises. Our traditional goal of high material consumption may well carry with it an unexpected price tag in the form of unpleasant complexities, stresses, and anxieties.

Thoreau's objective would instead be *freedom*; or better yet, what he simply called *life*: "The cost of a thing is the amount of what I will call life which is required to be exchanged for it immediately or in the long run."[14]

For many contemporary economists and businesspeople, this is indeed an odd theory of wealth, but it is one that is consistent with meadowlark values—including our personal and ecological health—values that Thoreau would defend both in his writings and in the way he lived. Indeed, it is a perspective that would force us all to look at our own lives and the larger economy in a new way: not as gross domestic product per capita, but something more like *life* per capita, if that could somehow be measured.

Thoreau was genuinely concerned for the economic welfare of his fellow citizens. But he also wished that we would take time to simplify our lives while enjoying the many planetary wonders in front of us and around us—and *not* wake up one morning, late in life, only to discover that we had never really lived.

Chapter 10

Wal-Mart Pond

*This curious world which we inhabit is more wonderful than
it is convenient; more beautiful than it is useful; it is more to
be admired and enjoyed than used.*

—Henry Thoreau

Recently while taking my morning walk, I caught a glimpse of a man
who was (and here I am afraid some of you will not believe me) none
other than our economic prophet, Henry David Thoreau.

Though he passed by me quickly, I noticed that his head was down,
looking, in fact, somewhat depressed as he strode by in his heavy boots
and long, black overcoat. Where was that cheerful, inquisitive naturalist,
poking into this, listening to that, letting nothing get by his legendary
powers of observation? Something, I believe, was bothering the man.

I felt duty-bound to catch up and ask: "Is it really you, *the* Henry
David Thoreau, Concord pencil maker, surveyor, poet, essayist, and
natural historian who retreated to Walden Pond over a hundred and
fifty years ago?"

"Yes, yes," he said, while giving me a strange look, as if he were per-
turbed about something.

"Anything wrong?" I inquired.

"Since you've asked, I'll tell you. To begin with, the other day I stepped
into one of your Main Street taverns. The owner invited me in to check

out her high definition television with Dolby Digital sound. 'It's the biggest LCD screen in town,' she said. The customers think it's awesome.'

"I then sat down to watch what she called her favorite 'soap opera' and what seemed to be a very loud quiz show. Terrible! Terrible! I told her, 'I'm sorry if I sound critical, Miss, but these programs confirm, for me at least, that the mass of men lead lives of quiet desperation.'"

"Henry, you've really got to be careful what you say to people," I said.

"Well, that wasn't all. That evening I returned to the same establishment and asked if anyone would like to go for a walk to listen to the spring peepers and watch the rising of the full moon. But no one seemed interested. In fact, one young gentleman glared at me and said, "Get real, dude. Like, can't you see there's game on?"

"I felt sorry for him," Thoreau continued. "It seems to me that a stereotyped but unconscious despair is concealed even under what are so-called games and amusements of mankind. Your cars, your television and movies, and what you call computers make things worse! Are they not all merely pretty toys which distract our attention from more serious things?"

"Most people," I said, "might argue that they are the most important advances since you wrote *Walden.* Come on Henry, weren't you awed by that high-definition TV?"

"Technically, my friend, it was impressive; but if all you watch are those puerile programs, then it would seem to me that your liquid crystal tele-machines are nothing more than an improved means to an unimproved end. As for your automobiles, see how they've disfigured, even destroyed what was once a lovely landscape! Everywhere you look—cars, roads, parking lots: Who is in control, you or your cars?"

Continuing his train of thought, Thoreau added: "If I had the opportunity to rewrite *Walden,* I would pay more attention to how the commercial interests, especially their advertising, have conspired to keep people—what should I say?—*stunted,* in their juvenile larval stage. The commercial interests clearly do not want people to grow up. One does not have to look far to see men and women wasting their lives with such toys and childish amusements!"

"Perhaps you are right," I said, "but most people here say that we have an excellent school system, and when their kids graduate they can work at the local Wal-Mart or the Mega-Mall in Minneapolis."

However, as I spoke, my friend was wistfully looking off into a distant woods; he then gestured toward the trees and quietly said, "Sir, what is important is a constant intercourse with nature and the contemplation of natural phenomena. The discipline of schools or businesses can never impart such serenity to the mind."

Turning to me again, he asked sharply: "Why do you need mega-malls or Wal-Marts?"

"Americans love to shop, I mean … er, we purchase products that make our lives more interesting, more comfortable."

"I'm not so sure," he countered. "Many of the so-called comforts of life are not only not indispensable, but positive hindrances to the elevation of mankind. Believe me sir, you don't need shopping malls."

Changing the subject, I asked if he had seen any meadowlarks about, as they seemed to be losing ground. Bullfrogs, too. Even our fireflies and leopard frogs were diminishing in numbers, I told him.

"No, I haven't. Indeed I am very sad to hear about such things. As for me, I am still searching for a hound, a bay horse, and a turtledove. Any chance you might have seen one of these?"

Actually, that morning I had seen a pair of mourning doves on a telephone wire, but I don't think that's what he meant. Besides, I didn't want to bring up the subject of long-distance communication, recalling what he said in *Walden* about the magnetic telegraph that would connect Maine to Texas. "Maine and Texas, it may be, have nothing important to communicate," he wrote.

Thoreau then asked me what I did for a living. "I'm an economist," I said. "I teach a little, write a little, sort of like what you did years ago."

"You're an economist? Perhaps you are responsible for the government income tax."

"Well, yes, I suppose economists had something to do with it, along with politicians."

With that, Henry Thoreau began to explain what was really on his mind, a worry that had distracted him to the degree that he wasn't able to write or even enjoy his walks anymore.

"The government is after me," he confessed. "They said that I would have to pay back taxes on all the royalties I've earned over the years from the sales of *Walden,* as well as my other poetry and essays."

"Tough problem," I said. "But I've got an idea that might work, especially for you. Explain to them that you want to take a poet's deduction for all your expenditures. You would therefore have no taxable income and hence no tax liability."

"Wait a moment. You're going much too fast for me. What is a poet's deduction? I confess, though, I like the sound of it."

"Okay. Take your shoes, Henry—"

"What do my shoes have to do with taxes?" he interrupted.

"Don't you see? The cost of your shoes is a legitimate business deduction, like the cost of, say, a farmer's silo or barn. Do you remember when you once wrote: 'How many a poor immortal soul have I met well-nigh crushed and smothered under its load, creeping down the road of life, pushing before it a barn seventy-five feet by forty, its Augean stables never cleansed.'"

"Yes, first chapter of *Walden,* I believe."

"What you didn't realize is that those uncleaned Augean stables are not completely bad: a farmer is allowed a business deduction for all his expenses, his barn included."

"Hmm … I think I'm beginning to understand."

"You might argue that anything a poet, a philosopher, indeed anything a writer like yourself purchases is part of operating his business, so to speak. That is, there is no separation between a poet's lifestyle in general and his or her writing in particular—those things from which they earn their income. Therefore *all* your expenditures can be deducted from your royalties. Yes, Henry David Thoreau, you can deduct your shoes—and everything else, too."

With that my friend began to brighten up.

"Extraordinary idea, sir. I'll pursue your poet's deduction when I next meet with the tax man. But now I must take my leave. I see it's the waking day's crepuscular hour, my favorite time of the day. Thank you, sir, and good-bye."

He sauntered off. (Did I detect a smile on his face?) I saw him go down the road a ways, then step off into a nearby meadow. Engrossed with something, he stopped, took out his journal and, I'm pleased to report, began writing again.

Chapter 11

Darwin's Finches
and Ford's Mustangs

The lucky individual that finds a different seed, or nook, or niche, will fly up and out from beneath the Sisyphean rock of competition. It will tend to flourish and so will its descendants—that is, those that inherit the lucky character that had set it a little apart.

—Jonathan Weiner

"Survival of the fittest!"

Consider the many times we've heard this expression applied to the business world. Other "Darwinian" phrases include: "finding a niche in the marketplace," "the struggle for existence," or the "extinction of a company or a product line." How easily the ideas and vocabulary of evolutionary biology flow into the world of economics and back again.

But how accurate is the analogy? Is Darwin's world of evolution by natural selection a workable metaphor for a business creating profitable product "variations" in the marketplace?

In one important sense—the method of creating variations—the business and Darwinian worlds are quite a bit different. Natural selection implies *random* variations of living organisms. In contrast, businesses develop products through *artificial* selection, that is, through conscious and deliberate decisions on the part of designers, engineers, market researchers, and their focus groups. Nature uses a "shot-gun" approach, inefficiently producing a large number of offspring, with some having an advantageous physical or behavioral trait that improves the chances of reproductive success. Their offspring, in turn, will then carry on that favorable trait, helping subsequent generations to survive. To see how this works in greater detail I would recommend Jonathan Weiner's excellent book, *The Beak of the Finch*. In it, Weiner describes the long-term studies of various species of finches living in the Galapagos Islands off the coast of Ecuador. The Galapagos studies suggest that it is relatively small variations—say in the depth or length of a finch's beak—that can make the difference in the survival of an individual bird, especially during times of environmental stress. Favored birds, in turn, not only survive but will be more likely to successfully reproduce and pass on their genes to the next generation.

If Darwinian dynamics were applied to business, an automobile company, for example, would have to manufacture thousands of slightly different models each year, hoping that one or a few might survive in the marketplace. Such a wasteful and expensive process would obviously be both inefficient and unprofitable.

Businesses must *condense* their selection processes by artificially preselecting good designs, then market-testing them in advance using a sample of potential buyers. Today's automakers utilize 3D computer modeling techniques to search for potentially marketable designs from millions of possibilities. Indeed, why manufacture (as nature does) inefficient variations when they can be winnowed down through intelligent designs and scientific market research techniques?

Once the selection process has narrowed the possibilities, however, then a business/biological analogy becomes more accurate. For example, if a company's product becomes successful, it attracts sufficient "resources" (revenues and profits) to keep it "alive," thereby guaranteeing its "reproduction" (continued manufacture) until there's a change in the overall economic "environment" (consumer preferences, manufacturing costs, competition, etc.).

These lessons were highlighted some forty-five years ago in Ford's epic Edsel failure and its Mustang success. The Edsel's development included no market research in the testing of stylistic variations. Although Ford put its Edsel into a potentially profitable niche (occupied at the time by Olds, Pontiac, and Buick), it projected a poor front-end design while early models suffered from substandard mechanical quality. Edsel's developers made an unforgivable mistake of offering a new and relatively untested push-button gearshift mechanism that was not only costly to produce, but suffered from an unacceptably high failure rate—nearly 50 percent in the first three months of sales! One could have predicted that, sooner or later, the "species" *Fordus edselus* would become extinct.

In contrast, the Mustang is still alive in the marketplace, projecting its familiar morphology (general body shape) after having gone through various transitional forms up to and including the Mustang of today. Both Mustang's name and styling had the advantage of market research starting with demographic studies that forecasted a bulge of relatively young car buyers, (the postwar baby boomers) ready to purchase their first car. A biologist might say that a new and viable niche was emerging.

For Ford, improved quality control would also be a key consideration. According to my father, Robert Eggert Sr. (who was Ford Division Manager of Market Research during this period), high reliability would be important not just for a new Mustang, but as a selling point in the used-car market, a key factor in maintaining consumer brand loyalty.

In addition, the well-known name—Mustang—was chosen via a carefully planned and deliberate selection process. In the spring of 1963 Ford tested some thirty-three names. Focus groups were then asked to rate each name by the criteria: "suitability as a name for the special car" and a more generalized "feeling for the name" while viewing a clay model of the car's design.

In reviewing the original focus group results, I learned that the least popular names were Carnelian, Calli, and Fangio. Lee Iacocca, then vice president of the Ford Division, pushed for Turino, a name that scored a little bit below average in both criteria. The name Thunderbird II did better, but not nearly as well as Panther, Dolphin, or Commando. Mustang, a name inspired by the title of J. Frank Dobie's book *The Mustangs* scored the highest.

How did the Mustang (in contrast to the Edsel) keep quality up and prices down? Here we see another intriguing analogy to Darwinian evolution. Consider again Darwin's famous finches: Studies suggest that the finch's evolutionary path takes place conservatively, that is, its underlying body (the "chassis") doesn't change much. Although variations take place throughout the entire body over many generations, there's little selective pressure to change the basics. According to the Galapagos studies, it is the small variations in the beak that appear to be the deciding factor in survivability—especially during periods of drought. Putting it in another way, the finch's basic "infrastructure" tends to be a reliable component of survival and hence requires little alteration over time. So how does this idea relate to the Mustang?

On this point, one might say Ford had an evolutionary insight. In a critical decision in 1962, Mustang's development team made a decision to use the relatively reliable chassis and drivetrain of an earlier Ford model (the Falcon). Evolutionists might therefore call the Falcon a "common ancestor" to the Mustang and to subsequent Ford models built on the Falcon chassis. The upshot was that the Mustang's base price ($2,368) could be kept relatively low. The car would also earn an enviable reputation for reliability since all the "bugs," common to new models, had already been corrected. It's intriguing to see how the title of a relatively obscure book (*The Mustangs*) helped one automaker go from a walk to a gallop, eventually making a profitable run across the 1960s economic landscape.

In summary, from bird beaks to body styles, to our own evolutionary journey through time, we live in a wonderful world of creative change, energized by forces of natural and artificial selection contributing to Earth's rainbow of diversity—plants, animals, and (just look around you) a variety of inventions conceived within the miraculous inner workings of the human imagination.

Chapter 12

Then the Sun Came Up:
Creation Myths and Mr. Darwin

The sun is rising. All the green trees are full of birds, and their song comes up out of the wet bowers of the orchard. Crows swear pleasantly in the distance, and in the depths of my soul sits God.

—Thomas Merton

Many public television viewers will surely remember that wonderful series *The Power of Myth*, featuring Bill Moyers' interviews with the famous mythologist Joseph Campbell. Among other things, viewers learned the following: although myths may not be factually true nor scientifically based, they have nevertheless provided our species with an infrastructure of meaning necessary for maintaining a cohesive culture over the generations. Mythological stories, Campbell argued, infused the collective mind with magnified emotional truths as they taught us about the origin of the universe, the nature of good and evil, and the deep, abiding complexity of the human condition. The *Power of Myth* has also made it easier for me to bridge for myself that canyon of misunderstanding between Darwinian evolutionists and biblical creationists.

To illustrate, let's first consider a Paiute Native American story entitled "Why the Sun Rises Cautiously,"[1] which involves a legend that uses an everyday natural phenomena to teach young people about socially harmful traits, including selfishness, foolishness, and a destructive tendency toward violence, all personified by an irascible rabbit who wants to get even with the Sun (Tab-e) for making his life miserable. Poor Cottontail, you see, has to suffer through the unbearable heat of a Utah summertime. I won't tell you the ending except to say that the story uses the *reluctance of the Sun to rise* to teach the rabbit (and the reader) important tribal values, including the difference between good and evil.

A second illustration from the early Mayan texts also highlights the importance of the rising sun. Here we learn about the so-called "First People" from the *Popol Vuh,* the sacred book of the Mayan Quiche. The first Mayans were known as "mother-fathers" who lived their lives in a perpetual dawn, before the advent of days and nights and the predictable movement of the sun across the sky. In a state of perpetual hunger, they lived in a kind of unnerving twilight zone, forcing the mother-fathers to wander around aimlessly in the darkness, with no sense of belonging to a place and with no conception of social order.[2]

So what did they do about it?

> In the midst of this suffering, the mother-fathers climbed up a mountain called Place of Advice, and there resolved to turn the mass starvation into an act of penance. Tohil and the other gods were moved at this and responded by ordering Jaguar Quintze and his companions to keep their sacred images safe.... And suddenly, the dawn began.... In their happiness, Jaguar Quintze and his fellows cried sweetly and burned incense in gratitude. *Then the sun itself came up.* As it did so, all the birds and animals rose up from the valleys and lowlands and watched the joyous spectacle from the mountain tops. The birds spread their wings to the sun's rays and the first human beings knelt in prayer.[3] [italics added]

Of course, such teaching myths that incorporate the importance of the rising sun are based on an indisputable fact of nature. After all, the sun does rise, doesn't it? Certainly all one's senses affirm it. You can *see* the sun rise in the east. You can *feel* it on your skin. Flowers warmed by a rising sun release fragrance; in this sense you can *smell* a rising sun. Birds know the sun rises in the morning and if you are fortunate enough to enjoy their songs (as did Thomas Merton, whose quote begins this chapter), you can practically *hear* the sun coming up. No question—the sun *is* rising!

The only problem is that the sun is *not* rising. It's essentially at a standstill in relation to the Earth. The sun remains fixed despite our forgetting 99 percent of the time that the Earth moves around the sun; our deep sensual/emotional truth, that the sun rises to meet us, persists. The scientific explanation, as Galileo unsuccessfully argued to the Catholic Church over three hundred and fifty years ago, is an *invisible truth* lurking in the shadowy world beyond one's senses. Indeed, it is a truth usually less important on a day-to-day basis than our common perception of seeing the sun rise in the morning.

Still, every once in a while, I try to make an effort to experience the reality of the dawn brightening by envisioning a fixed sun *awaiting* our great blue-green sphere as it slowly turns—as the Earth pulls its mountains, oceans, rivers, cities, and all its children along and slowly circles down, down into the light of the sun. It is an interesting sensation, but it's not the perception that has emotionally energized thousands of years of stories, legends, and time-tested mythologies.

In recognizing the importance of mythological/emotional truths, I can now better understand the creationists' point of view and their passionate argument against evolution. They too are immersed in an important and powerful mythological truth: that God literally fashioned the stars, the Earth, and all the animal and plant species pretty much as we see them today. Like the creationists, I too am often reluctant to acknowledge that my own ancestry descended from a common ancestor of primates. Indeed, while attending a lecture by a leading biblical creationist, I saw a sign with a simple but very thought-provoking question: FROM GOO TO YOU??

My ego whispered: "Ridiculous … no way!" And within that frame of mind, it seemed obvious to me (like the rising sun is obvious) that the broad implications of Darwinian evolution were too odd, too strange to be true; indeed, my personal identity and sense of what it means to be human was at stake. Yet just as I can accept the scientific fact of a moving Earth and stationary sun, I am now convinced that in the vast scientific studies and experiments in the fields of genetics and physiology—not to mention the fossil record—biological evolution is the best explanation of how we got here.

Humans and humanlike species evolved, I believe, like all other plant and animal species, through the process of natural selection. And just like the fixed sun/moving Earth example, I now see human evolution as a kind of invisible truth, a shadowy history painstakingly discovered over a hundred or more years of scientific endeavor. (It is no coincidence that the late Carl Sagan and Ann Druyan titled their book on this subject *Shadows of Forgotten Ancestors: A Search for Who We Are.*)

And yes, every once in a while, I will hold up my hand and think: it is plausible that the curvature of my fingers was, over millions of years, shaped by tree branches, or the arch of my foot was carved upon the African savanna. Years ago, when my appendix was removed, I recall asking the surgeon the purpose of the appendix. It was a vestigial organ, he said, that was important to our vegetarian ancestors long ago. (Given the deaths of so many children from ruptured appendices, one would have to wonder why God would ever consider designing humans with such a deadly deficiency.) My doctor also stressed that I had to take my full dose of antibiotics; if I didn't, I would be contributing to the problem of antibiotic-resistant strains of bacteria—another illustration of biological change via Darwinian natural selection.

This conviction was further reinforced when my daughter and I were visiting Zion National Park in Utah. While walking one of the trails along the river, we came across an interpretative sign explaining how a local species of snail had changed under the impact of geological forces.

Steering clear of the words Darwin, evolution, or natural selection, the sign simply summed up what science has learned from the fossil record of the snail *Petrophysa zionis*:

> Its ancestors probably were pond snails in the old, sluggish Virgin River. Uplift of the land made the river too swift and muddy for their food plants to grow. Food did grow in wet spots on the walls of the deepening canyon. Snails which had happened to have a smaller shell and larger foot could cling to the wall better. They survived more often than the others. The environment favored continued reduction in shell and enlargement of foot. Thus the present form is quite different from the ancestral pond snails.

Sounds plausible to me. And if there's evolution of snails why not of *Homo sapiens*? Indeed, there are times when I'm in a mood, an expansive sensibility, as it were, when I feel a deep psychological satisfaction in being part of a long-term evolutionary relationship, a kinship with all other living things; it's not at all frightening, but really quite wonderful.

But that's not my day-to-day experience. Just as I go about my mornings enjoying the "fact" of a rising sun, I have no trouble *feeling* the emotional/mythological "truth" Joseph Campbell so beautifully outlined years ago. During these moments, I too gravitate toward the power of myth and generally accept, with that same comforting conviction as my creationist friends, that "our kind" is unique from other evolutionary experiments in life's long history—despite scientific evidence to the contrary.

PART III

On Cosmic & Spiritual Evolution

Chapter 13

Celebrating Our Cosmic Journey

Why should I feel lonely? Is not our planet in the Milky Way?
—Henry Thoreau

Who hasn't felt a shiver down their spine contemplating the creation, the vastness of the cosmos? Or asked themselves: *How did it all begin?* and *Where do we fit within the ongoing evolution of the universe?* More often than not, these questions are rekindled in our thoughts and conversations as we step out under the bright stars of a dark night.

Indeed, I recall so well that mild summer evening years ago when our nine-year-old daughter and I walked hand-in-hand to the back of our property. On that unusually dark and beautiful night, we made our way to a secluded part of our land. Earlier, I set up a small telescope in a relatively flat, unobstructed viewing area. We then pointed our telescope toward the lovely constellation of Lyra, the "Harp" configuration of stars between the constellations of Cygnus and Hercules.

Next, we took a peek at Lyra's unusual Ring Nebula, a donutlike gray-green wisp of fluorescence or, some might say, a faint puff of smoke from some far-off pipe. What we saw was actually a dying star some twenty-two hundred light-years away. Astronomers tell us that Lyra's ring is a bubble of hot gas expanding ever outward—a gentle but final shrug of a relatively small star that was once much like our own sun. We were, in a sense, witnessing a grand preview of our own stellar future.

Of course, our sun's solar swelling and superheated ring-puff will occur between one and five *billion* years from now—plenty of time for good digestion, a long, long life, plus sufficient geological time for millions of future generations of Earth-bound species, including ourselves. But eventually our home star will change into what astronomers call a "red giant." It will swell and burn with intensity. Its expanding heat and searing bubble will burn Earth's precious skin of green and atmospheric blue. It will vaporize rivers and oceans alike, boil away every stream and splash of puddle.

"But," my daughter asked, "Will people be able to live? Would we have to wear space suits? Could we move to Pluto?"

I was impressed with her strategies for survival. Of course, it may be possible to extend life on another planet or a moon within our solar system. But sooner or later, our Sun's hot ring and its inevitable burnout will leave scant hope for life-forms within this planetary neighborhood. As one astronomer described it, "... the Sun will be a cold, black-dwarf governing a retinue of fused and hard-frozen worlds orbiting in a darkness lit only by the light of the distant stars."[1]

In the meantime, what do we do? Perhaps we should simply share the beauty, share the evening's friendship and wonder while witnessing the moment, *this* moment. That night my daughter and I chatted about our feelings and life's meaning. We mixed into our hour some science and silence while experiencing the deepening darkness and relishing the night's enchantment. Also that August evening, we saw some meteors. My companion counted eleven. Excitedly she nudged me—"Look, look!"

As we packed up our telescope, we made a date to go out again. But next time we would observe not star destruction, but stellar creation. We promised each other that come winter, we would take a peek a Orion's famous nebula, a zone of the night sky that astronomers have described as a "stellar nursery." In observing Orion's bright dust cloud, one can actually witness infant stars in the making, baby stars sparkling through the blue-green glow of Orion's galactic mist. Such are some of the ongoing creations of our ever-evolving universe.

My daughter and I would both make one last glance overhead, taking in the unearthly stillness while admiring the dark and deepening beauty. Again, who has not sensed those large questions coming on as he or she stood, so small, so insignificant, under the sweep of stars and the mystery of the night?

If I could, I would like to find out where we came from, to follow back that old trail of universal time and visit of some of the landmarks of our cosmic history. The ideal? To make familiar the sequences that brought us to this moment of consciousness, then to invite this history into the mind and heart, not with fearful strangeness but with understanding and affection, as familiar as our own home, or perhaps like C. S. Lewis' version of comfortable familiarity: "soft slippers, old clothes, old jokes, and the thump of a sleepy dog's tail on the kitchen floor."[2]

What actually happened then, in the interval from that original emptiness to the moment of us sharing these thoughts, or me sitting at my desk tapping the keys of an old Royal typewriter while enjoying the distant trill of a resident field sparrow?

Both modern science and also some of the ancient creation stories believe that in the beginning, there was a pause. It might help to try and imagine pure space, pure emptiness. It's interesting to note that there are large zones in our night sky where there's practically nothing at all: cosmic voids, they're called. Two voids that have been closely studied are the Boötes Void (named after the constellation that depicts a mythological herder) and the one in Coma Berenices ("The Hair of Berenice"). You might try to find these constellations on some dark night in the spring. Then relax (take your time), and imagine the great gaps within. Can you somehow sense the pure space and great emptiness just before the universe began?

To get into the mood, I sometimes look through my telescope at an "empty" zone of the night sky, away from the great masses of stars. For me, at least, this is a starting place. I look and look and look, taking in the magnified circle of magnificent blackness. On these special nights I recall the quotation from the *Tao Te Ching*, the Chinese philosophical text written in the fourth century BC by Lao Tzu:

> The Way is a void
> Used but never filled;
> An abyss it is,
> Like an ancestor
> From which all things come …
> Whose offspring it may be
> I do not know;
> It is like a preface to God.[3]

Again I put my eye to the eyepiece, looking into empty space. Within the ring of ultrablackness, I can sense the quiet:

> There is a being, wonderful, perfect;
> It existed before heaven and earth.
> How quiet it is! How spiritual it is! It stands alone and does
>   not change,
> It moves around and around but does not on this account
>   suffer.
> All life comes from it.
> It wraps everything with its love as in a garment …
> I do not know its name.[4]

Consider too the many Native American creation stories, some of them surprisingly similar to Lao Tzu's description of modern cosmology. One of my favorite legends involves an original being called Maheo whose mood, it was said, could determine the state of the universe:

At first there was nothing. In the beginning there was nothing in all of time and space. Only was there darkness and Maheo. If Maheo was silent, then the Universe was silent. If Maheo was still, then the Universe was still.... All around Maheo was nothingness and silence, age upon age.[5]

Then Maheo began to realize the great power he had, the power to actually create. From that insight, he reasoned that "power is nothing until it has been used to do something." Thus armed with both power and insight, Maheo concluded it was time for action:

He took all of time, past and present and future, and gathered it in one hand. Into his other hand he gathered all space. With these in each hand he clapped. A great clap it was, greater than thunder. For this clap was the first sound ever heard in the Universe.[6]

Continuing the story, we learn that from that first "clap,"

came all things, and everything from which all things could be made.... Stars came flying out of his hands like sparks from crackling wood in a fire. Everywhere did the stars fly out and continue to fly out and burn today everywhere across the night-time sky. This is how time began and all things began to be made.

To a modern astronomer, Maheo's "clap of creation" is again amazingly similar to the Big Bang theory of the beginnings of the universe (with the addition of some familiar audio/visual effects: "like sparks from crackling wood in a fire"). Consider too the Old Testament's creation story of Genesis 1:3. The biblical description brings to light an important detail, conforming nicely to recent scientific theory. Recall that on the first day of creation, before the Earth had form, "God said, Let there be light: and there was light."

Physicist Chet Raymo, author of numerous books on astronomy, believes that the Big Bang was actually misnamed. Instead of "The Big

Bang," he suggests "The Big Flash," an event some 13.7 billion years ago consisting of "an infinitely dense and infinitely hot seed of energy"[7] coming essentially out of nothingness. And as the universe fed upon its elementary diet of light and gravity waves, the primeval cosmos literally flowed from physical matter into light and back again into matter. Of that stupendous, creative moment, cosmologist Gary Bennett writes:

> Packets of energy called photons raced through the early universe.... In a sense the universe at this state *was* light.... Although the temperature had cooled a lot since the inception of the universe less than a millionth of a second before, it was still enormously hot—hundreds of times hotter than a detonating hydrogen bomb. At these temperatures, matter emerged as elementary particles when photon collided with photon. Einstein's famous equation $E = mc^2$ beautifully documents this early era when energy and matter flowed back and forth interchangeably.[8]

And what happened after this grand opening event of our universe? Professor Raymo states rather simply (I detect here almost a yawn, as if the really hard part was over): "the universe was off and running."[9]

After a millisecond of extreme rapid expansion ("era of inflation"), astronomers mark a point (about four minutes after the Big Bang) where the universe "cooled down" to approximately a billion degrees, while its elemental composition consisted of approximately 75 percent hydrogen and 25 percent helium.

Virtually all the heavier elements such as carbon and oxygen would thereafter be manufactured in the process of star births and star deaths, that is, in the interiors of stupendous fireballs and planetary nebulae (such as Lyra's Ring Nebula), and most importantly, within the titanic explosions of supernovas, intense zones of radical destructions and fused creations, of atoms compressed into heavier and heavier elements. Hydrogen fuses into helium and on to carbon, oxygen, silicon, and iron, ever recycling, ever evolving.

So where do we look? In what direction of the night sky did this stupendous "Big Bang" event take place? In actuality, we are of the Big Bang and are currently coevolving with it after nearly fourteen billion years. In response to the question, "where did it take place?" we learn that the Big Bang "occurred everywhere … space itself came into existence with the Big Bang." Indeed, the remnants of the original creation event can still be heard today via microwave radiation that "hums" smoothly and evenly from each and every part of sky. Unable to pinpoint a single direction of the source, I confess to some disappointment, as if I had run into an invisible barrier in investigating a crucial detail of my family history.

However, the next stage of cosmic evolution does offer greater possibilities for gaining a feeling for, and connection to, our early universe. Gary Bennett continues his description of the beginning moments:

> As hydrogen and helium spewed forth from the primeval fireball, instabilities in the material formed and grew. Vast clouds of hydrogen and helium, each billions of times more massive than the Sun, fell together under the pull of gravity to make protogalaxies. Inside the newborn galaxies, turbulent regions of gas coalesced under gravity into stars.[10]

Indeed, we can detect, even "see" these very young, massive galaxies, and within their cores or centers we find highly energized radiation sources astronomers call quasars. Quasars appear to be fantastic powerhouses, stupendous beacons of radiation dating back to just two or three billion years after the Big Bang. This makes the telescopes that detect them equivalent to scientific time machines, witnessing the universe as it existed four-fifths of the way back to its explosive birth. Though quasar beginnings are still somewhat mysterious, there are some interesting theories about their origins.

Some astronomers suggest that they were formed as ancient galaxies collided (not an unexpected event, as the universe was more tightly bound up at the time). Furthermore, it's believed that each of these "quasi-stellar" objects contains one or more black holes, or large gravity whirl-pools that tug on and pull in gas, distort space itself, and thereby capture even light waves that pass nearby. Yet just before the final descent of matter and light into the blackness-of-no-return, some ultrahot elements (heated by friction) beam out powerful waves of radiation like a final "cry" before the doomed matter disappears into the swirling vortex.

Astronomers may disagree about some of details of the Big Bang and its aftermath, but there is little argument over what we can see when we step out on a clear, moonless night. Nearby, in time and space, we have friendly stars, beautiful stars easily accessible with a pair of binoculars or simply a bend of the neck. And those lucky enough to experience a night sky without light pollution can enjoy that lovely river of light called the Milky Way.

In his book *Armchair Astronomy*, British author Patrick Moore explains that it would be theoretically possible for a single star to escape from a galaxy such as the Milky Way:

> Once beyond the galactic halo, a star would be beyond the limit of detection … particularly if it were a star no more luminous than the sun. We can visualize the sky as seen from a planet moving round such a star. The night sky would be virtually blank; nothing would be seen apart from dim glows in the extreme distance. It would seem decidedly lonely, and I think we must be grateful that our Sun is not a solitary wanderer in the space between the galaxies.[11]

"Decidedly lonely …" but as we know, we do have an intimate galactic neighborhood, a cosmic home visible as a lovely, creamy-white trail of countless specks of light seen overhead on a moonless night. In our Milky Way galaxy, there are some two hundred billion stars in addition to the sun! And not only can we easily see our galaxy, but we also know something about its size and spin. We are lucky to live in an age when astronomers can, with reasonable accuracy, pinpoint our solar system's position within the galaxy's vast, wheellike superstructure.

To bring the Milky Way, symbolically at least, into close proximity, one could begin with a cup of hot water and a spoonful of instant coffee. Once you submerge the crystals, give the liquid a clockwise spin. Within seconds, you've created a miniature galaxy out of a conglomeration of bubbles. A coffee galaxy will usually consist of a central core of densely packed bubbles and well-defined spiral arms that swirl about against a backdrop of inky blackness.

Assuming you make one of these tiny galaxies, and if it has two or three spiral arms, you have now re-created a surprisingly good representation of the Milky Way. Miniature coffee galaxies are perhaps two or three inches across. The Milky Way, in contrast, is some one-hundred thousand light-years from edge to edge. (Recall that a light-year is the distance that light can travel in a year's time—approximately six trillion miles.) In comparison, the closest galaxy that's similar in size to our Milky Way—the great galaxy of Andromeda—is a little more than two *million* light-years away.

As we visualize the Milky Way swirling through space, we might then be curious and want to know: exactly where do we reside in respect to the galaxy's central region and flowing arms?

Telescopic data indicate that our sun's location is neither in the center nor on the very edge of the Milky Way. Our galactic arm, the Orion Arm (or "Spur"), is between the inner Sagittarius Arm and the outer Perseus Arm. And within the Orion Arm, the sun is approximately twenty-eight thousand light-years from the galactic center. Or, it could be said, our solar system's "suburban" location is roughly three-fifths of the way from the galaxy's nucleus to its outer edge.

Perhaps on some cold winter evening you will find yourself taken in by the Milky Way's great river of stars coursing across the sky. If so, try to find the Charioteer constellation of Auriga (near the Pleiades, or "Seven

Sisters" constellation). Since our solar system is located in the inner part of the Orion Arm, when you look at Auriga, your line of sight will be looking toward the thick middle region of our spiral arm's river of stars (opposite the galactic center). If, however, you look toward the bright star Sirius (the "Dog Star"), your galactic view will be directly into the *outer* section of the Orion Arm's tail.

In late summer you'll have another opportunity to orient yourself, only now your line of sight will be directed into the interior zones of the Milky Way galaxy. For example, when you look at the constellation Cygnus, the "Swan" (easily seen in August or September), you'll be looking toward the *inner* part of the Orion Arm, toward the stellar "roadway" that would lead round to the Milky Way's central core. Our solar system is, in fact, moving in Cygnus' direction as we circle the galaxy's nucleus.

Now look toward the constellation Sagittarius (the "Archer"), which is perhaps best seen from a lawn chair on a clear, moonless night in August. (From overhead, North American observers can follow the Milky Way's starry "river" down to the southern horizon.) As you skim the horizon, you may not see the well-defined archer, but something more resembling a teapot.

Now if you would happen to shoot a cosmic arrow toward the spout of the teapot, your arrow would travel through trillions of miles of space—through dark, obscuring dust clouds and massive star clusters, and finally (some twenty-eight thousand light-years away), your arrow would penetrate the center of the Milky Way's nucleus, the mysterious heart of our galaxy. Because of the intervening dust and gas, the Milky Way's central core is all but invisible—even to the most powerful optical telescopes. Yet it can be "seen" with telescopic instruments that are capable of measuring infrared, X-ray, ultraviolet, and other forms of high-level energy. Thus, on an imaginary journey to the Milky Way's center, we would eventually come upon "... a monstrous pulsing heart for the Galaxy, a core of violence that recapitulates the violence of the creation itself. The nucleus of the Milky Way Galaxy is apparently the site for cosmic convulsions on the grand scale, perhaps a place where countless suns are swallowed up by a massive gravitational black hole."[12]

Every once in a while it is helpful to experience a true sense of place—even on a galactic scale. Of greatest importance is the fact that we reside at a relatively safe distance "in the suburbs," so to speak, away from lethal pulses of radiation from the central core. But wouldn't it be interesting if there was some way to get a photograph, or perhaps construct an image of what the Milky Way might look like from a distance, to somehow capture the galaxy's elegant form and inherent beauty in its entirety? Given the hundred-thousand light-year span of our galaxy, humans may never see the Milky Way from such a distant vantage point. Yet it is relatively easy to take a look at a close neighbor—the great Galaxy of Andromeda—a spiral galaxy surprisingly similar to our own in size and shape.

To find Andromeda's fuzzy congregation of stars, it helps to have a star chart on hand as well as a pair of small binoculars. If you want to increase your chances of success, try viewing Andromeda on a moonless night in mid- to late September, when mosquitoes have disappeared and darkness arrives relatively early in the evening. First, can you find the North Star via the Big Dipper? Next, find the constellation Cassiopeia, located on the other side of the North Star from the Big Dipper. Cassiopeia's most conspicuous feature is a compact group of stars in the shape of a "W." Note that the bottom side of that "W" consists of two "pointers" directing your line of sight even further to the east. Using the upper pointer, sweep your binoculars to the right until you come upon our sister galaxy as a faint, fuzzy smudge. You've just located Andromeda.

As you look through your binoculars, Andromeda may not be a very spectacular sight. However, you can magnify Andromeda not just through your eyes, but also in your mind. Consider Andromeda's three hundred billion stars. How many planets might it have? And what varieties of life and other amazing creations and fascinations? Consider that its light has traveled approximately two million years before reaching the Earth. And too, that the light from our Milky Way of two million years ago (from the era of some of the earliest humanlike creatures) is now reaching Andromeda, making it easy to see (in our imagination) the Milky Way's soft galactic glow.

Enjoy Andromeda! Consider her swirl and inner secrets. Imagine the billions of stars within a single galaxy and then step back to consider the billions of galaxies that are at this very moment unfolding to the music of creation and the evolving harmony that began with the Big Bang. Now return again to the Milky Way (*our* Milky Way), and home in, if you can, on our solar system. Can you make out that lovely blue-and-white, cloud-swirled world below?

I have often wondered what it would be like to be an astronaut, to see the Earth from such a vantage point in space, to be a lucky observer from above our planet's neighborhood: how would it feel? Perhaps Louise Young, in her book *The Blue Planet,* said it as well as any, reflecting on the beauty, delicacy, and indeed, the very miraculousness of it all:

> In the photographs of the earth from space, the planet looks like a little thing that I might hold in the hollow of my hand. I can imagine it would feel warm to the touch, vibrant and sensitive.... Beneath the mobile membrane of cloud and air are a storehouse of splendors and a wealth of detail. There are rainbows caught in waterfalls, and frost flowers etched in window panes, and drops of dew scattered like jewels on meadow grass, and honey creepers singing in the jacaranda tree.[13]

And finally, let us return to solid earth, to our neighborhood, and to the warmth and comfort of knowing we are home.

Chapter 14

Life!

Tao is in an ant, in a blade of grass, in a roof tile, in dung ...
you'll not find it apart from the ten thousand things.
                                                    —Chung Tzu

Not too far from our family home here in west-central Wisconsin, a small miracle comes our way ever so rarely, rising up out of a bed of pine needles from our pine-oak and jack-pine savanna soils. I drop to my knees.

The atmosphere's quiet. The pine-duff layer seems soft and moist to the palm of my hand. There, in the low morning sun, is a fist-sized ring of tiny mushrooms—*Panaeolus foenesecii*—all eleven of them brightened by fresh sunlight beaming through the pine boughs. Each is vigorous, healthy—full of *mirth,* it seems to me.

Bending down, I touch one with my cheek: cool in temperature, rubbery to the skin, it's packed with a newborn life force. Closer to the ground now, I suddenly see small strands of spiderwebs rippling to my right, each fluttering in ruffled waves of rainbow color.

Consider for a moment the favorable confluence of historic and current conditions—biological, geological, atmospheric—first to conceive of this scene and then to make it into a solid fact: air temperature, nighttime humidity, morning sun, perfect pine-duff moisture, plus all the necessary mushroom-producing nutrients. A delicate combination of chemistry and biology—of DNA imperatives hereby springing up *life!,* now spreading out before me in wind-puffed riffles of color. Lost in wonder, as if submersed in a dilation of time, I sense old kinships in these familiar forms—an antique creativity summoning up newfound energies. From primordial conditions to such beauty, *How,* I wonder, *did the universe do it?*

And you and me as well: are we not equal partners of such processes, popping up out of rare circumstances, a genuine gift arising from equally improbable events? Are we not, like the mushrooms, exquisite outcomes of evolutionary forces from a truly creative universe cooking up new flavors of recombinant matter, of compounds heated and shaped by fields of physical energies—both weak and strong—over unimaginable quantities of time? And what about Earth itself?

In their book *Rare Earth,* Peter Ward and Donald Brownless argue that our planet, especially its complex life, is likewise an extremely improbable event. If true—and their argument seems persuasive—our species and its cultural and technological status may be the only example of our kind within galactic range. Like the little mushrooms, Earth's unique characteristics are a result of a confluence of improbable yet favorable factors.

Why would complex life-forms living on other living Earths be so rare? First, our species required a planet that was situated in precisely the right galactic neighborhood; one, as we learned in the previous chapter, safely distanced from the intense and deadly radiation beaming out of the massive black hole at or near the center of the Milky Way. We also needed a planet residing in an older galaxy, one that had been around sufficient time to recycle materials into birthing stars and out of dying novas and supernovas—each titanic explosion a cosmic factory for fusing simpler, lighter atoms into heavier elements, each transformation creating the critical ingredients for life as we know it.

Next, we needed a planet with sufficient quantities of water and a planetary mantle liberally sprinkled with life-supporting compounds. We needed a planet with atmospheric oxygen and a stratospheric ozone membrane; like the gentle hands of a devoted mother, Earth's precious ozone layer protects all her terrestrial children from the sun's deadly ultraviolet radiation.

Equally important, we would require what astronomers have dubbed a "Goldilocks Planet" which, like the Little Bear's porridge, was not too hot (like Venus), or too cold (like Mars). Recall that wonderful moment, the one that will make the children smile, in "The Three Bears" story:

> And then she [Goldilocks] went to the porridge of the Little Wee Bear, and tasted it, and that was neither too hot nor too cold, but just right, and she liked it so well, that she ate it all up, every bit![1]

Earth is, in fact, the only planet we know of that enjoys an average global temperature within a comfortable, life-supporting range between the freezing and boiling point of water. The authors of *Rare Earth* remind us of the importance of Earth's relatively large moon, which helped stabilize our planet's tilt and life-supporting atmosphere. A comparable planet to the Earth would also have to have a sizable sibling, a planetary big brother with Jupiter-strength gravity sufficient to absorb dangerous interplanetary projectiles. Without Jupiter, our planet would have been hit by comets and asteroids far too often and thus would have suffered too many mass extinctions over the past half-billion years.

Yet ironically, some jolts and planetwide buffetings were necessary. According to the Rare Earth hypothesis, the evolution of humans required episodes of ice ages and also some (not too many) earth-shattering impact from above. Consider the great dinosaur extinction of sixty-five million years ago that allowed furry, shrewlike mammals of the night to get a foothold and then, over millions of years, occupy new and safe daytime niches around the globe.

Equally important, we required a planet that had the capacity to stir things up from below through plate tectonics. Moving plates not only recycle essential chemicals, but continuously create new habitats and niche opportunities which, over long periods of time, reshape bodies and behaviors into new species through natural selection.

How lucky we are! Lucky to reside on a planet with tortoise-paced moving continents. Indeed, lucky to inhabit a possible one-in-a-billion "rare Earth" finely tuned for birthing such a wide range of biodiversity.

That morning was thus graced by mushrooms and resplendent spider-webs fluttering in the wind and a unique rare Earth species-consciousness invoking feelings of wonder and a renewed sense of planetary precious-ness. But there was also a feeling a cosmic *loneliness,* of meandering about in a minor key, as it were. Who could not also feel a deepening fear or dread that our requisite care and tenderness toward our planet has not always been what it should, that our rare Earth has been so ravaged by human violence, climate destabilization, and ecosystem disfigure-ment? That our technologies and Earth-consuming appetites have so altered the biosphere that many of those things we hold on to with such affection are now beginning to fade, seep away, indeed slip forever from our fingers.

Consider the planetwide deforestation and growing number of bleached-out coral reefs. Consider global warming, ozone thinning, and the worldwide shortages of fresh water or the well-documented amphibian declines and deformities (and the extinction of that beauti-ful, shimmering Golden Toad of the rainforests of Costa Rica). With any species extinction—such as the passenger pigeon, dodo, great auk, heath hen, or dusky seaside sparrow, to name a few—one should con-sider essayist Mark Walter's observation that although death is the end of life, "extinction is the end of birth."[2] Holmes Rolston, arguing along similar lines, writes that "extinction kills ... the soul as well as the body" and that "to superkill a species is to shut down a story of millennia and leave no future possibilities."[3]

We must also think about the world's bourgeoning population—over six billion souls with all their material needs plus their pent-up desires—which, if current trends continue, will be half again as large within a generation. Consider too the clear-cutting of national forests and Asian mountainsides or the growing severity of worldwide droughts, while elsewhere torrential rains and tragic mudslides cascade down into cities and villages.

Where, one might ask, are our rare-Earth religions or a rare-Earth economics, or evidence of rare-Earth political sensibilities circling the globe? Where is our commitment to a rare-Earth covenant, if you will, flowing from the influential realms of society, from science and religion, economics and business, and a politics dedicated to protect the creation from plunder and defilement?

Surely many of the early spiritual traditions were informed and enriched by a deeper level of ecological consciousness and transmitted to their followers a heightened appreciation not only of the environment but of a deep, interconnected, harmonic chord of all life. I think, for example, of that great prophetic verse from the Taoist spiritual classic, the *Tao Te Ching,* a verse that beautifully captures all the delicacy, fragility, and indeed the vulnerability, of the natural world:

> Those who would take over the earth
> and shape it to their will,
> never, I notice, succeed.
> The earth is like a vessel so sacred
> that at the mere approach of the profane
> it is marred
> and when they reach out their fingers it is gone.[4]

Or consider a passage in the final book of the Bible, a revelation startling perhaps to those who may have never considered this book as a powerful environmental document: "... that thou should give reward unto thy servants the prophets ... and should destroy them which destroy the earth."[5] Or listen to what may be the greatest deep-ecology values statement of all time—when the God of Genesis paused to contemplate everything newly created and proclaimed that "... it was *very* good."[6]

Or consider the voice in the whirlwind reminding Job that when God had planned the Earth there was a moment of great merriment when, as the poet wrote, "the morning stars burst out singing and the angels shouted for joy."[7] (Is it so difficult to share that same unabashed elation arising from such a creative undertaking?) Or how the Psalmist cried out so boisterously, so joyfully, his high praise for the natural world:

> O Lord, how manifold are thy works!
> In wisdom hast thou made them all:
> The earth is full of thy riches.[8]

Consider too the story of Noah as a moral teaching which, according to biologist Calvin DeWitt, is nothing more or less than the world's first Endangered Species Act.[9] DeWitt reminds his readers that Genesis 6–9 highlights God's command that Noah prevent the extinction of all creatures, *both economic and uneconomic, no matter what the cost.*[10]

And didn't Jesus admonish his listeners (as did St. Francis, Henry Thoreau, and John Muir) to simplify their lives while warning of the love of money and materialism that distracts us from spiritual development? The early writings and scriptures of Islam and Hinduism are equally resolute in condemning greed and the worship of wealth. Buddhists add an additional element of environmental awareness in the view that humans are not separate from the creation, but intimately part of and interdependent with it. In his book *The Sun My Heart*, Zen Buddhist teacher Thich Nhat Hanh illustrates this vital relationship when he asks his readers to consider "the immense light we call the sun":

> If it stops shining, the flow of our life will also stop, and so the sun
> is our second heart, our heart outside of our body. This immense

heart gives all life on earth the warmth necessary for existence, along with carbon dioxide from the air, to produce food for the tree, the flower, the plankton. And thanks to plants, we and other animals can live.... We cannot begin to describe all the effects of the sun, that great heart outside our body.[11]

Elsewhere on the subject of Buddhism and deep ecology, he asks us to:

Look into the self and discover that it is made only of non-self elements. A human being is made up of only non-human elements. To protect humans, we have to protect the non-human elements—the air, the water, the forest, the river, the mountains, and the animals.... Humans can survive only with the survival of other species. This is exactly the teaching of the Buddha, and also the teaching of deep ecology.[12]

One's growing awareness of this Earth/human interdependence may then become a touchstone for one's behavior, lifestyle changes, and, of course, one's day-to-day choices. Yet, for some reason, this traditional wisdom has become enfeebled, like a far-off candlelight obscured by great and growing distances—as we race forward embracing the novelty of technology, bottom-line obsessions, and a far-ranging infectious consumerism—making all too many of us unwitting contributors to the slow but steady degradation of this beautiful planet and its countless wonders.

So who is responsible and why? I would, of course, like to point my finger outward toward corrupt governments and greedy transnationals, or perhaps at the advertisers and the entertainment industry whose visions of paradise are unalloyed materialism fueled by profits and exponential growth. Yet as I now realize, I too am co-responsible, and therefore my finger (if I am honest) points right back toward me.

Chapter 15

Co-Responsibility

When we try to pick out anything,
We find it hitched to everything
else in the universe.

—John Muir

I recall so well that evening when, in the bloom of spring, my wife and I took a leisurely walk down a nearby nature trail.

It was all ours—for the seeing, the listening, and here and there, for the sweet smelling of the plum blossoms hanging over the path. On the edge of trail we found fresh floral offspring of botanical natives whose ancestors settled here after the last glacier, their living relatives now deeply rooted, as if with a sense of peace and belonging: juneberry, trout-lily, and, growing out of a wet bank, fronds of fern unfurling.

Soon we passed a prairie remnant and further on discovered marsh marigolds blooming in a sparkling bog. (We have our own marsh-golds, like the sacred lotus of India, flaring their color up and out of the bog mud and into our hearts.) Nearby, skunk-cabbages sprout elephant ears for leaves, a yellowthroat warbler scolds *whichity ... whichity,* a catbird meaows from behind a bush.

We pause. What's that high-pitched, haunting trill—as if a thin string of beads had been lofted out of a wet meadow, then transmuted magically into sound? Ah, it's the music of little toads who, like other lovers on the trail, offer their large affections to the efflorescence of the evening, their yearnings to the ripeness of spring.

Turning the bend, we saw something odd, clearly out of place. Somewhere in the vast rooms of our brain, there's a recognition center alerting us to novelty which, like an unexpected special news bulletin interrupting soothing music, arouses our curiosity. This object was white, a little less than a foot in length, and surprisingly straight. As we got closer, curiosity modulated into confoundedness. Nothing that I know of in nature is so smooth, so precisely linear.

The mystery object was a plastic straw that had been thoughtlessly tossed into the wetland. My wife Pat fished it out. It was mostly white, but on closer inspection, we noted that it also had a thin red stripe down one side and a yellow one down the other. Some of its plastic had been chewed off and discarded. *Not for me!* some critter must have thought to himself. Nor for us either, this artifact from the world of fast foods, this offspring of chemical engineers, oil wells, tankers, pipelines, plastic extrusion processes, and robotic packing machines.

Oh, the delicacy of the day, its hushed, prayerlike moment—now so rudely interrupted! Instantly, from eye to brain, feelings of disgust entered the judgmental room of my mind and soon rippled down into my body, briefly diminishing the color, the music, the wonder and sparkle of the moment.

Days later, I would reflect on that evening. I would wonder why I accept, with little thought or feeling, much greater disfigurement of the natural world as I drive through our cities and suburbs. Or, for example, not react when I dispose of my own trash, week by week, each plastic bag destined for some invisible landfill.

I confess to living day to day mentally predisposed to destructive states of denial, and also to a gross numbing of my native sensitivities, of accepting wide-ranging forms of social and environmental blight as normal—light pollution, exhaust pollution, subtle chemical pollution, endless sprawl—and also of doing very little to prevent the cancers, the children's asthma, or the mercury in fish, to name just a few transgressions of my values, of my covenant with our rare Earth.

If I could only be more aware of my actions and what I am consuming, I would understand that I too am *co-responsible* for the poisons, for animal and plant extinctions, for global deforestation and the planet's slow but inexorable climate change. As Buddhist writer Thich Nhat Hanh put it:

> … the most important precept of all is to live in awareness, to know what is going on, not only here, but there. For instance, when you eat a piece of bread, you may choose to be aware that our farmers, in growing the wheat, use chemical poisons a little too much. Eating the bread, we are somehow co-responsible for the destruction of our ecology.[1]

Lately, for example, I have been thinking about my driving habits. Consider the fact that my wife and I drove to the nature trail. Each gallon of gasoline, when combined with atmospheric oxygen, adds nearly twenty pounds of carbon dioxide into the air. Indeed, on a recent fill-up (about a week and a half's worth of driving), I consumed approximately 10 gallons of gas for 320 miles. In driving the 320 miles, I was responsible for adding about 200 pounds of carbon dioxide to the atmosphere. Furthermore, my own records indicate that I've averaged some 10,186 miles per year over a four-year period (a little less than the U.S. average of 11,300 miles). At 32 miles per gallon, that's 318 gallons per year, or over 6,200 pounds (over 3 tons) of carbon dioxide!

In addition, my driving has probably contributed something to urban ozone pollution close at hand, and also to acid rain that may be damaging lakes and forests further away. In his thought-provoking book, *The Dying of the Trees,* author Charles Little comments on the industrial and transportation pollutants responsible for killing off red spruce groves in the Green Mountains of Vermont: "The agents of their demise are invisible chemicals produced a thousand miles to the west without a by-your-leave or apology."[2]

The author also details how distant atmospheric pollutants have altered the forest's soil structure and chemistry, leaching heavy metals into the topsoil. These spruce stands, according to soil scientists, may never grow back. From spruce forests to childhood asthma activated by urban ozone to disastrous oil spills, there's surely a vast array of related collateral damage to our excessive consumption of oil.

Sometimes when I complete a litany of social and environmental damage from my driving, a student will ask if I don't feel guilty. I try not to, I always say, because guilt often dissipates over time and is eventually replaced by a comfortable state of moral amnesia. Instead, I believe that the principle of co-responsibility should become a tool or perspective for understanding, a kind of force field for truth, in the same spirit perhaps as the great religious insights. As poet Matthew Arnold once wrote about the Sermon on the Mount, Jesus was not engaging in what Arnold called "stiff and stark external commands" but in lessons that "have the most soul in them; because these can best sink down into our soul, work there, set up an influence, and form habits of conduct."[3] So too with the principle of co-responsibility, as a method of gaining a deeper understanding to help shape our personal and collective actions.

Another example from my own home economy involved a purchase our family made a number of years ago. In the summer of 1991 my wife and I put down new kitchen flooring; on the advice of our local building supply store, we dutifully purchased the recommended underlayment: sheets of a thin, smooth plywood called *lauan*. Lauan is one of the varieties of Philippine mahogany of the genus *Shorea*. These four-by-eight-foot panels originated from trees that can reach a height of one hundred and fifty feet with a circumference of eighty-five feet or more.[4]

I can easily visualize these ancient forests—from their underground roots to their overarching canopies—forests replete with unique, diverse, and fully functioning ecosystems including, of course, wonderful groves of gentle mahogany behemoths, trees larger in circumference than even the great redwoods of California. (It would, for example, take some twenty children to put their collective arms around a single trunk of the largest of these giants.) Such an image by itself should have given us pause in purchasing lauan mahogany for our kitchen subflooring.

Imagine our shock and dismay when, a few months after the floor was completed, we discovered that the Philippine island of Leyte (a major source of lauan) had suffered massive flooding, death, and destruction traced to large scale clear-cutting of Philippine mahogany from the island's mountainous slopes. With little foliage to break the energy of some six inches of rain from tropical Hurricane Thelma, plus the absence of root systems that normally anchor the topsoil, an estimated twenty-one million cubic yards of earth washed down the mountainsides on the fifth of November, 1991, creating a ten-foot-high wall of water, mud, and debris—all cascading into Leyte's Anilao River valley—and then continued to rage through and scour the heart of the island's largest city, Ormoc. By the end of the week, some six thousand residents had died, tens of thousands were homeless, and millions of dollars worth of crops had been ruined. Two days after the flood, *New York Times* reporter Seth Mydans pieced together various on-the-site observations[5]: "Residents of Ormoc said the floodwaters, preceded by a great roar, uprooted trees, flushed cars down the streets and ripped wooden houses from their foundations."

Why did it happen? When Lito Osmena, governor of the nearby Philippine island of Cebu, presented his explanation, I wondered if our family too didn't play some small role in this tragedy:

The forests are gone and I guess over-logging is one of the major causes.... That area gets several typhoons a year but they never resulted in something like this, and I think it is because the forests are gone. Illegal logging, with the complicity of local politicians and military officers, has recently become recognized as a major environmental problem in the Philippines. Forest cover is being stripped from the hillsides and erosion is degrading the land.

After the great flood, other eye-witnesses reported the following:

> The captain of an inter-island vessel, Porfirio Labugnay, interviewed in Cebu, said: "I saw bodies and animals, cows, pigs, and household appliances floating in the sea off Ormoc city."
>
> "People were in a panic," said Demetria Go, a 48-year-old resident. "They were scampering into the streets. Some children climbed up trees yelling for help." People were screaming as they ran from their houses.

Like individual drops of rain (dollar by dollar by dollar), these monetary pulses, when added up, swell into a powerful river—a great global force that's beyond any individual's or group's control. Add in greed, poverty, political corruption; add in clear-cutting shrouded from view and muffled by distance, and you now have a confluence of events ripe for human and biological tragedy on a massive scale.

Leyte's 1991 flood was not an act of God, but truly an act of humans—consumers, loggers, sellers, politicians, and all the persuasive advocates for unregulated free trade. Indeed, after the tragedy of Leyte, I understood for the first time what author Helena Norberg-Hodge meant when she wrote:

> The ever-expanding scope and scale of the global economy obscures the consequences of our actions: In effect, our arms have been so lengthened that we no longer see what our hands are doing. Our situation exacerbates and furthers our ignorance, preventing us from acting out of compassion and wisdom.[6]

After the Leyte disaster, I'm also able to better understand what environmentalists call an "ecological footprint," a concept (like co-responsibility) that forces us to recognize our own social and environmental responsibilities beyond their immediate visual space. One's ecological footprint, for example, can be defined as the approximate amount of land a person requires for housing, transportation, waste disposal, food, and so on. Rough calculations indicate that each North American, on average, uses between eleven and thirteen acres of productive land to meet their material requirements.[7] (An average person in India uses approximately *one* acre.) After Leyte, the environmentalists' observation, "… if everyone on Earth had the same levels of consumption as North Americans, we would need *three planets* to satisfy our demand,"[8] seems not only plausible but might well be a thought or image that we can, as Matthew Arnold wrote, "sink down into our soul, work there, set up an influence, and form habits of conduct."

In thinking about these issues, I sometimes get depressed. I feel as if I were submerged in an ocean of commercialism, drowning in a for-profit culture. It's to my left, my right, it's above me and below me. The bottom line is, well, The Bottom Line. It's in our language, it's in our schooling philosophy (to get a good job), it's in nearly every media niche saturated with commercialized entertainments along with their daytime and nighttime flood tide of marketing messages. It's in the hourly report: The Dow Jones Industrials are up (or down). It's in politics bought and sold, it's in retail stores that never close, it's in electronic televangelist churches promoting material prosperity. Indeed, it seems to be deeply embedded in many of our work and family issues: stress, debt, overwork, road rage, loss of free time, deterioration of community, teenage self-image issues, eating disorders, and environmental alienation. More than likely you contribute to this pervasive capitalist culture and no doubt, so do I. Another example? I checked out our family's mutual-stock fund and discovered that we had inadvertently invested in the world's largest fast-food company (remember the plastic straw?), a major transnational forest products corporation, and three of the world's most profitable consumer retailers.

Who, I wonder, is not co-responsible for those powerful economic forces which, when revealed, seem to sadden the heart and wound the soul; forces, like the great flood of Leyte, that diminish creation and irreversibly damage the beauty and diversity of our rare Earth?

Time perhaps for quiet reflection, a stillness, or Sabbath[9] if you will, to meditate on what we have done to our planet—not to generate anguish or guilt, but for spiritual nourishment through greater insight and gentle understandings.

Equally important—are we not *co-responsible for a future* which, on a planetary scale, must be sustainable? I do believe that an ecological consciousness will be forthcoming when we are capable of listening to the variegated voices of the natural world and can respond appropriately with our sciences, our time-tested cultures, and equally important, our cherished religious and spiritual values. My metaphor for this balance comes from the botanical world, an image familiar, I'm sure, to all: like a flower—or, one might say, a flowering!

Chapter 16

Like a Flower:
A Meditation on Balance

Difficult and easy balance each other.
Long and short complete one another.
High and low rely on each other.
Pitch and tone make harmony together.

—Lao Tzu

Stillness.

Mindfulness. And now, like the roots of a flower absorbing a gentle rain, can you become *porous,* opening up to the creative power that drives the universe and feeling fully connected to its manifestations? For our species, these manifestations might be metaphorically likened to a flower—four petals with four different colors.

First, the color brown, representing our cosmological and biological past. Each of us contains atomic structures formed in the life-and-death rhythm of countless stars. In addition, each of our cells' DNA is packed with deep-time animal histories—from Cambrian chordates, from fish to amphibians, from reptiles to fist-sized mammals, from arboreal apes to savanna-dwelling *Homo erectus.* Evidence of our common past is contained in our shape, our organs, our limbs—indeed, in the very structure of our brains. This first petal represents our species' physical and psychological origins grounded in nature and Earth's long history. It is surely a manifestation of who we were—and in addition, is also connected to our present psychological well-being.

Those, for example, who live in bubbles of man-made technologies may find it difficult to reconnect to this ancient part of ourselves—to experience what biologist E. O. Wilson calls *biophilia* [1]—an innate attraction to and psychological need for bonding with nature, its landscapes, ecosystems, and its communities of plants and animals.Cocooned in our cars or cooped up in our classrooms or office cubicles, or simply consuming hours of our waking days wandering through an unnatural wasteland of prepackaged electronic entertainments, we may be allowing our vital connection to nature to atrophy, thereby suffering from a peculiar loneliness, a vague unsettling or alienation, even depression. Children especially need large chunks of unprogrammed, spontaneous time in nature to discover landscape niches, to "practice the wild," [2] as poet Gary Snyder once called it. Essayist Diane Ackerman agrees: "We need a lively, bustling natural world so we can stay healthy.... We need it to feel whole. We evolved as creatures knitted into the fabric of nature, and without its intimate truths, we can find ourselves unraveling." [3]

Biophilia is but perhaps a new term paralleling older themes embedded in writings that go as far back as second-century naturalist Pliny the Elder (who, for example, believed that the only virtuous life was one lived in balance—*ratio*—with nature[4]), the Bible, British poet William Wordsworth, John Muir, Aldo Leopold, and, as we noted earlier, the nineteenth-century writer and naturalist Henry David Thoreau.

Recall Thoreau's comment that "there could be no black melancholy to him who lives in the midst of nature and has his senses still." [5] And what better definition of *biophilia* than Thoreau's description of an inner musical counterpoint between himself and his feathery neighbors:

Instead of singing like the birds, I silently smiled at my incessant good fortune. As the sparrow had its trill, sitting on the hickory before my door, so had I my chuckle or suppressed warble which he might hear out of my nest.... I am no more lonely that a single mullein or dandelion in a pasture, or a bean leaf, or sorrel, or a horse-fly, or a humblebee.[6]

Consider too Wisconsin teacher and naturalist Aldo Leopold. Despite Leopold's training as a "bottom-line forester," his understanding and appreciation of the natural world would eventually evolve toward values beyond economic utility, even beyond the aesthetic dimension: "Our ability to perceive quality in nature begins, as in art, with the pretty. It expands through successive stages of the beautiful to values as yet uncaptured by language."[7] Like Thoreau, Leopold would become more and more critical of an economic system geared to short-term gain and essentially out of balance with ecological values.

As a writer and conservationist, John Muir also dedicated his energies to "do something for nature and make the mountains glad," and like Thoreau, Muir could dissipate despondency and depression by taking periodic pilgrimages into the wild. My favorite Muir quote, however, is not from his legendary mountain or glacial hikes, but from a moment of relaxed repose, when he stretched out between two rivers and a flowering grassland:

Here is a calm so deep, grasses cease waving ... wonderful how completely everything in wild nature fits into us, as if truly part and parent of us. The sun shines not on us, but in us. The rivers flow not past, but through us, thrilling, tingling, vibrating every fiber and cell of the substance of our bodies, making them glide and sing.[8]

In the same spirit as these American naturalists, major Judeo-Christian figures—Moses, John the Baptist, Jesus—apparently felt that same urge to seek spiritual nourishment in wilderness settings including rivers, lakes, mountains, and deserts.

For Bartholomew I (Ecumenical Patriarch of the Eastern Orthodox Church), any destruction of the natural world should be considered a sin. Bartholomew, in the spirit of the great poet-naturalists, says that "human beings and environment form a seamless garment of existence, a complex fabric that we believe is fashioned by God."[9]

In addition, environmentalists applaud Jesus' (and St. Francis') core values of simplicity, not so different from Thoreau's. Related to this ethic is one of the most famous sayings in the Bible, "the love of money is the root of all evil."[10] Surely no ecologist could have fashioned a better metaphor for a modest and sustainable lifestyle of what might be called "contented gratefulness" than Jesus' metaphor of the lilies of the field (Matthew 6:28): "Consider the lilies of the field, how they grow; they toil not, neither do they spin: And yet I say unto you, that even Solomon in all his glory was not arrayed like one of these."

More than likely, the above flower is what botanists today call the crown anemone *(Anemone coronaria),* still common in northern and central Israel.[11] As I type these words it is early May in Wisconsin, that time of year to check out our own version of the genus *Anemone.* In the nearby woods I should have no trouble finding our own wood anemone *(Anemone quinquefolia);* friend of the woodfern and starflower, neighbor to the nodding trillium and wild lily-of-the-valley, the wood anemone rises only a few inches above the leaf litter. Simple yet exceptionally beautiful, each flower is adorned with showy white sepals and a globular white stamen. (John Greenleaf Whittier once praised this diminutive beauty, shimmering in the lightest of breezes: "… wind-flowers sway/ Against the throbbing heart of May."[12]) And like the biblical crown anemone, our anemone is also lovely without effort and "fairer than Solomon in all his glory."

Native to its woodland setting, *Anemone quinquefolia* has evolved a perfect ecological fit to its environment, enjoying a balance with other native plants and animals of its woodland economy. In such a stable setting, natural checks and balances prevent any single plant from taking over, as happens elsewhere with aggressive, invasive species that have gained a tenacious foothold in North America, including the kudzu vine, spotted knapweed, purple loosestrife, and European buckthorn, to name but a few. Finally, our wood anemone has created a miniature "sustainable economy," humbly adding leaf and flower litter to the woodland floor, thereby contributing small but reliable quantities of humus to the topsoil each year.

Another way of looking at Matthew 6:28 is that Jesus' flower metaphor brings balance to the otherworldly Christian message—reminding us that we must also bring our attention *back to Earth*. Indeed, I believe that any spiritual tradition that does not "harmonize Heaven and Earth" as the Chinese say, or emphasize the Holy Spirit along with the spirit of the valley, or that forgets about wild flowers, vernal pools, mudflats, and soils, will become as unbalanced as an economics devoid of ecological values. The Old Testament Psalmist who writes so beautifully of the heavenly dimension:

> Because thou hast made the Lord, which is my refuge,
> even the most High, thy habitation[13]

perhaps should have added an equally true nature-oriented counterbalance:

> Because thou hast made nature, which is *also* my refuge,
> Even unto the most low, thy habitation too.

If our Earth connection is colored brown, let's color our *spiritual* potentialities yellow. Yellow represents both the energy of the Holy Spirit in Christianity and the Tao's "great being," described as:

Wonderful, perfect …
All life comes from it.
It wraps everything with its love as in a garment …
I do not know its name.[14]

It also represents Buddhism's Great Love *(mahakaruna)* and the infinite mercy of Allah[15] and Islam's golden rule, strikingly similar to that of Christianity and Judaism: "No one of you is a believer until he desires for his brother that which he desires for himself."[16]

"While we know not definitely what the ultimate purport of life is," wrote the Zen Buddhist, D. T. Suzuki, "there is something in it that makes us feel infinitely blessed in the living of it and remain quite contented with it in all its evolution."[17] Yellow is the mystical awareness ballooning up and around American poet Walt Whitman as described in his poem, "Song of Myself":

Swiftly arose and spread around me the peace and
    knowledge
that pass all argument of the earth.... And I know
    the spirit of
God is the brother of my own.[18]

Next, consider the important dimension of *traditional culture,* the third petal of our flower; let's color the cultural influence red. Our cultural heritage is the learned social sphere we live in, influencing us all day to day, year by year, informing us not only how to survive but how to enjoy a richer existence. If the culture's influence is positive, among other things it assists us in diminishing our ego, making it possible to grow through family and friendship intimacies as well as through wider circles of social belonging.

Traditional cultural practices also tend to be finely tuned to their local landscapes, far more so than the "popular cultures" of today. Similar to the ecological "fit" of the wood anemone, traditional cultures fit into their specific landscapes and, over time, evolved sustainable economic practices. For thousands of years, horticultural and hunter/gatherer cultures integrated ecological and spiritual ethics through ceremony, cosmologies, mythologies, taboos, stories, songs, dances, food sharing, and other customs. Thus we discover unique and sustainable *culturescapes* in all their variation and richness.

Consider, for example, the traditional horticulturists and herders of Ladakh, a district in northern India, beautifully described in Helena Norberg-Hodge's study, *Ancient Futures.* In her book, we learn about a way of life that has maintained an exquisite balance between a people and its local resources, a balance that has been aided and informed by Buddhist practices and principles including interdependence, co-responsibility, and a reverence for life.

As a professional economist, I was impressed when I read about Ladakh's age-old adaptations over the generations, and consequently its success in solving fundamental economic survival problems. The model in Ladakh has therefore become for me a useful, indeed, an inspiring touchstone to compare and contrast with my own free-market capitalist economy. For Ladakh is not a growth economy but a *stable* economy, successfully fitting into the natural limits of its boundaries without radically altering the land or destroying its resource base. Ladakhians live in an environment that provides not only economic sustenance but a landscape where one can discover plant and animal teachers as well as time-honored sacred sites—storied places of love and belonging.

In contrast, global capitalism reshapes the land (without the love or belonging). Not fitting into the landscape, capitalism reconfigures landscapes based on the dictates of unlimited growth and profit—giving rise to industrial farmers, sulfide miners, stream straighteners, road wideners, wetland drainers, and forestry clear-cutters, to name a few.

Within the "modern" urban sector of Ladakh, Norberg-Hodge also describes some of the tragic environmental and psychological consequences of Western globalization, education, and tourism. In the span of only a couple of decades, she witnessed an increase of relative poverty,

social isolation, greater levels of air and water pollution, disempower-
ment (especially among women), and an increase in ethnic tensions
between the Buddhists and Muslims.

As once traditional cultures are undermined by the seduction of
modernization beamed out by the ubiquitous global media—billboards,
movies, radio, TV—young people feel that irresistible tug toward Western consumptive lifestyles. Shunning traditional ways, the younger generation is, however, not completely adapted to the modern economy
either, lacking sufficient income to keep pace with Western material
habits. They're floating in a kind of no-man's-land—unsuccessful "twoworlders"—between traditionalism and Western "middleclassism." Without roots in either world, without a reliable religious/cultural infrastructure of meaning and belonging (yet eager for the fruits of consumerism),
many become resentful and, not surprisingly, sometimes fall prey to
scapegoating and militant propaganda.

After reading Norberg-Hodge's account of Ladakh's recent stresses
and struggles, I felt that we too, while seemingly integrated into a modern consumer economy, also suffer from some of the same social and
psychological symptoms of land and culture uprootedness, and therefore
experience similar alienation, though in perhaps less obvious ways, as
the populations of developing countries. "And so we have before us the
spectacle of unprecedented prosperity," farmer/poet Wendell Berry once
wrote, "... but in a land of degraded farms, forests, ecosystems, and
water-sheds, polluted air, failing families, and diminishing communities."[19] In fact, any society, I believe, that trades in a balanced ecological
and spiritual ethic for one obsessed with materialism and fueled by economic discontent will find itself severed from its roots. In a pop-culture
environment saturated with advertising, prepackaged entertainments,
and competitive consumption, we will often lose our sense of place,
and direction along with it. Therefore, we should rediscover our own
cultural "red-petaled rootedness," to become intimate with our land-

scapes and our watersheds; to learn, if we can, the land's histories, stories, and songs; to be acquainted with its geology, its plants and animals; to revive, if possible, local crafts and folklore, or play out rituals that help us become more native to our place; to feel nourished, like the residents of traditional Ladakh, by a living landscape with our own special places of love and belonging.

In his book *Miracle Under the Oaks*, Richard Stevens describes some of the accomplishments, disappointments, and joys of a Chicago-based prairie restoration group. In reading about their experiences, I can make out the beginnings of a true local culture, informed by common purpose and group solidarity, united by rituals (for example, burning the prairie in the springtime), and guided by "elders" (those who've mastered the art and science of ecological restoration). In a revealing comment, one member of the group said:

> What's happening here is that Europeans are finally becoming Americans. We are developing an intimate relationship with this continent, and the landscapes of the continent, and we're doing it using the science of ecology, a product of our own culture....[20]

There is no reason why one cannot strive to become what might be called a "successful two-worlder," not only by becoming rooted in one's locality, but also by being comfortably at home within the blue petal (our fourth petal)—that is, *our broad culture of learning*, including the fruits of past and present human accomplishments: the sciences, literature, music, arts, and languages. This "liberal learning" dimension also implies tolerance of differences and of being open to diverse perspectives, plus an appreciation of technologies that have proven to be democratic, humane, ethical, and sustainable. I see this petal colored the pastel blue of a predawn sky before sunrise, reminding us of a new day, energizing a passion to learn within the liberal spirit of free inquiry.

This broader culture, embracing the fruits of many civilizations, is our species' relatively new source of kinship and belonging, shining brightly through time and space. Despite human greed and destructiveness, despite unpardonable violence, the great achievements of humankind make me glad to be a member of that quirky tribe, *Homo sapiens.*

Like a flower. And now perhaps a miracle for our species' future: a *flowering*? But then it would be no more of a miracle than the native prairie, or the lowly wood anemone, or the towering pine, or the bluebird that just dived into the grass outside my window, or the song of a meadowlark; or the sound of a raindrop or the virtuosity of a sunbeam.

Eventually, of course, new conditions arise and old ones disappear. At one moment, the wonders of creation take on one face, then another, and another. It was therefore not surprising that when I later returned to the mushroom site, I discovered that virtually all of the mushrooms had disappeared. *Pfffft* … gone! Nearby was a fern, a fragment of a blue jay feather, some decaying pine needles, a tuft of green moss, bits of bark, rabbit dung, and a pinecone half stripped to the core. But the mushrooms were nowhere to be seen.

Likewise, I can see my own life like a flower—now compact, coiled, ready for growth—and, eventually, my death, like the corolla relaxing its tension, petals letting go, and its various elements disintegrating into a great expansiveness ever outward. My brown "petal" will break down, precisely like the mushrooms. One's physical body disappears into the grass, into the soft moss, and down into the roots of the trees. In the mind of a naturalist, death is simply the painless and beautiful merging back into the earth. Toward the end of his life, John Muir wrote that he saw death as nothing more than the quiet voice of nature, a "kind nurse, whispering … come, children, to bed, and get up in the morning—a gracious Mother calling her children home."[21]

Similarly, the philosopher David Abram writes that indigenous peoples understand death as entering a different dimension of life, of existing within a new sphere of influence:

… death initiates a metamorphosis wherein the person's presence does not vanish from the sensible world (where would it go?), but rather remains as an animating force within the vastness of the landscape, whether subtly, in the wind, or more visibly, in animal form.[22]

Inherent in this view is the fact that the body dies, yes, but something still remains, as tenderly described in the following African poem informing us that "those who are dead are never gone,"

> They are there, in the thickening shadow.
> The dead are not under the earth.
> They are in the tree that rustles,
> They are in the wood that groans.
> They are in the water that runs.
> They are in the water that sleeps …
> They are in the breast of the woman.
> They are in the child who is wailing.[23]

Of course, biologically speaking, our children become part of our continuation, where the parent's germ cells transmit living genetic material into the next generation. Yet this continuation comes at the cost of the body's death. Indeed, according to cell biologist Ursula Goodenough, death is, in the larger scheme of things, essentially a "bargain made and trade-off accepted in return for making it possible to evolve complex organisms of various shapes, sizes, and modalities of behavior (including, of course, ourselves)." In her book *The Sacred Depths of Nature*, Goodenough explains the difference between our *somatic* cell function (providing us with bodies that strategize for survival and reproduction and are subject to change through the living/dying process of natural selection), and our *germ* cells, which live on into future generations. In response to the question, *Does death have meaning?* Goodenough suggests an answer that is not only scientifically accurate, but optimistic as well:

Well, yes, it does. Sex without death gets you single-celled algae and fungi; sex with a mortal soma gets you to the rest of the eukaryote creatures. Death is the price paid to have trees and clams and birds and grasshoppers, and death is the price paid to have human consciousness, to be aware of all that shimmering awareness and all that love.[24]

Next, the red and blue petals unloosen their tensions and radiate outward too. They are manifested in the form of our contribution to the health of our family, local community, and broader culture as well as to the local landscape: the cultural contribution involves parenting, teaching, mentoring, politicking, defending wildlife, or perhaps restoring a prairie, a watershed, a woodland, a degraded wetland or estuary. In this sense, we are all "ancestors to generations still to be born,"[25] as Native American writer Gerard Tsonakwa put it. And like the potential of any action (such as a single, simple act of kindness), the local ripples ever outward into broader zones of uncharted times and places. Revising the popular dictum, "Act locally, think globally," one could also say, Act locally *as if it mattered* globally.[26]

The yellow petal (spirit) also dissipates. But to where? (Surely it is an adventure worth looking forward to.) Do we enter a great void, or perhaps experience rebirth, as the Buddhists believe? Or does our consciousness merge, as some Native Americans believe, with the energy of the Great Spirit?[27] Or perhaps the Kingdom of Heaven? Or are our souls mysteriously united with the supreme reality of Brahman?[28]

Out of the flow of our life and death, out of our modest receivings and givings, out of our physical bodies manifested here and yet destined to move on, Chinese philosopher Lao Tzu drops his own tantalizing hint: "… that all eventually will come to Tao, as streams and torrents flow into the sea."[29]

Endnotes

Chapter 2: What's Wrong with Capitalism?

1. "American Gridlock," by Phillip J. Longman; *U.S. News & World Report*, May 28th, 2001.

Chapter 3: A Compensatory Ethic

1. See Bill McKibben's "When Words Fail: Climate Activists have Chosen a Magic Number," Orion Magazine, July/Aug 2008, p. 18-19. For more information on this topic, please check the web site www.350.org.

Chapter 5: High Jumping

1. George A. Sheehan, *Dr. Sheehan on Running* (Mountain View, CA: World Publisher, 1975), p. 190.
2. Eugen Herrigel, *Zen in the Art of Archery* (New York: Vintage, 1971), p. 41.

Chapter 8: Craftsmanship and Salvation

1. Elizabeth Drew, *Poetry: A Modern Guide to Its Understanding and Enjoyment* (New York: Dell, 1959), pp. 19–20.
2. Robert M. Pirsig, *Zen and the Art of Motorcycle Maintenance* (New York: Bantam, 1974), p. 91.
3. Henry David Thoreau, *Walden* (New York: Bramall House, 1951), p. 348.

Chapter 9: Simplify, Simplify: Henry Thoreau as Economic Prophet

1. Thoreau, *Walden*, p. 19.
2. Henry David Thoreau, *The Journal of Henry David Thoreau*, ed. by R. Torrey, F. Allen (New York: Dover, 1962). Journal entry from July 5th, 1852.

3. *Walden,* p. 66.
4. *Walden,* p. 66.
5. *Walden,* p.68.
6. *Walden,* p. 148.
7. *Walden,* p. 337.
8. Walter Harding, *The Days of Henry David Thoreau* (New York: Dover, 1982), p. 286.
9. *Walden,* p. 106.
10. *Walden,* p. 106.
11. *Walden,* p. 29.
12. *Journal,* July 19th, 1851.
13. *Walden,* p. 86.
14. *Walden,* p. 45.

Chapter 12: Then the Sun Came Up:
Creation Myths and Mr. Darwin

1. William R. Palmer, *Why the North Star Stands Still* (Springdale, Utah: Zion National History Publishers, 2003), p. 25–29.
2. Tony Allan and Tom Lowenstein, *Gods of Sun and Sacrifice* (London: Duncan Baird Publishers, 2003), p. 47.
3. Allan and Lowenstein, p. 48.

Chapter 13: Celebrating Our Cosmic Journey

1. Daniel Whitmire and Ray Reynolds, "The Fiery Fate of the Solar System," *Astronomy,* April 1990, p. 29.
2. C. S. Lewis, *The Four Loves* (New York: Harcourt Brace Jovanovich, 1960), pp. 56–57.
3. Lao Tzu, *The Way of Life,* trans. by R. B. Blakney (New York: American Library, 1955), p. 56.
4. K. L. Reichelt, *Meditation and Piety in the Far East* (New York: Harper & Bros., 1954), p. 56.
5. This story, narrated by Kiowa/Caddo tribesperson Mary Bombadier, was taken from *Legends in Stone, Bone, and Wood,* by Tsonakwa and Yolaikia (Minneapolis: Arts and Learning Services Foundations, 1986), p. 14.
6. Tsonakwa and Yolaikia, p. 14.

7. Chet Raymo, *The Soul of the Night* (New York: Prentice Hall, 1985), p. 46.
8. Gary Bennett, "Cosmic Origins of the Elements," *Astronomy,* Aug. 1988, p. 18.
9. Raymo, p. 47.
10. Bennett, p. 20.
11. Patrick Moore, *Armchair Astronomy* (New York: Norton, 1984), p. 128.
12. Raymo, p. 102.
13. Louise B. Young, *The Blue Planet* (Boston: Little Brown, 1983), p. 266.

Chapter 14: Life!

1. E. Johnson, E. Sickels, F. C. Sayers, eds., *Children's Literature* (Boston: Houghton Mifflin, 1959), p. 74.
2. Jerome Walters, "The End of Birth," *New Age Journal,* Jan/Feb. 1994, p. 65.
3. Walters, p. 65.
4. Lao Tzu, *The Way of Life,* trans. by Witter Bynner (New York: Capricorn Books, 1944), p. 43.
5. Revelation 11:18.
6. Genesis 1:31.
7. Job 38:37; *The Book of Job,* trans. by Stephen Mitchell (New York: Harper Collins, 1987), p. 79.
8. Psalms 104:24
9. This phrase was used in Calvin DeWitt's lecture, "Good News for the Land," Eau Claire, Wisconsin, April 10th, 2000.
10. Calvin B. DeWitt, *Earth-Wise* (Grand Rapids, MI: CRC Publications, 1994), p. 52.
11. Thich Nhat Hanh, *The Sun My Heart* (Berkeley: Parallax Press, 1988), pp. 66–67.
12. Thich Nhat Hanh, *The Heart of the Buddha's Teaching* (New York: Broadway Books, 1998), pp. 126–127.

Chapter 15: Co-Responsibility

1. Thich Nhat Hanh, *Being Peace* (Berkeley: Parallax Press, 1987), p. 65.

2. Charles E. Little, *The Dying of the Trees* (New York: Penguin Books, 1995), p. 35.

3. Matthew Arnold, *Essays in Criticism,* ed. by S. R. Littlewood (New York: MacMillan & Co. 1969), p. 173.

4. B. J. Rendle, *World Timbers,* vol. 3 (London: Ernest Benn Ltd., 1969), p. 44.

5. All quotes are from Seth Mydans' article "More than 2000 Die as Floods Swamp Towns in the Philippines," (*New York Times,* Nov. 7, 1991, A1 & A8).

6. Helena Norberg-Hodge, "Economics, Engagement, and Exploitation in Ladakh," *Tricycle: The Buddhist Review,* Winter 2000, p.115.

7. Eben Fodor, *Better Not Bigger* (Gabriola Island, BC: New Society Publishers, 1999), p. 24.

8. Fodor, p. 24.

9. See reflections on the Sabbath in Abraham Joshua Heschel's *The Sabbath* (New York: Farrar, Straus and Giroux, 1951), p. 6.

Chapter 16: Like a Flower: A Meditation on Balance

1. Edward O. Wilson, *Biophilia* (Cambridge: Harvard University Press, 1984).

2. Gary Snyder, *The Practice of the Wild* (New York: North Point Press, 1990).

3. Diane Ackerman, "Finding a Time Pool," *Audubon,* Jan/Feb, 2002, p. 49.

4. Kenneth Parejko, "Pliny the Elder's Environmental Ethic," (a presentation at the conference "Ecology, Theology, and Judeo-Christian Environmental Ethic," Feb. 22, 2002 at Notre Dame University).

5. Henry David Thoreau, *Walden* (New York: Bramall House, 1951), p. 148.

6. *Walden,* p. 128, 154.

7. Aldo Leopold, *A Sand County Almanac* (London: Oxford University Press, 1949), p. 96.

8. Joseph Cornell, *Listening to Nature* (Nevada City, CA: Dawn Publications, 1987), p. 42.

9. Sparlha Swaby, "The Venice Declaration: A Spiritual Imperative for Earth Care," *Earthlight,* Summer 2002, p. 6.

10. 1 Timothy 6:10.

1 1. Timothy Coffey, *The History and Folklore of North American Wildflowers* (Boston: Houghton Mifflin, 1993), p. 10.

12. Mrs. William Starr Dana, *How to Know the Wild Flowers* (New York, Dover , 1963), p. 6.

13. Psalms 91:9.

14. K. L. Reichelt, *Meditation and Piety in the Far East* (New York: Harper & Bros., 1954), p. 56.

15. Matthew S. Gordon, *Islam* (New York: Doubleday, 1956), pp. 3–4.

16. Quoted from the Sunnah in the *Old Farmer's Almanac,* 1992, p. 261.

17. D. T. Suzuki, *Zen Buddhism,* ed. by William Barrett (New York: Doubleday, 1956), pp. 3–4.

18. Walt Whitman, *Leaves of Grass* (New York: Paddington Press, 1970), p. 14. From "Song of Myself," #5.

19. Wendell Berry, "The Idea of a Local Economy," *Harper's Magazine,* April 2002, p. 16.

20. Richard Stevens, *Miracle Under the Oaks* (New York: Pocket Books, 1995), p. 16.

21. Linnie Marsh Wolfe, *Son of the Wilderness: The Life of John Muir* (Madison, WI: University of Wisconsin Press, 1945), p. 348.

22. David Abram, *The Spell of the Sensuous* (New York: Pantheon Books), p. 16.

23. Quoted from Knowledge Products' audio tape, "The Religion of Small Societies" (Nashville: Carmichael & Carmichael, Inc., 1994), tape 1, side 2.

24. Ursula Goodenough, *The Sacred Depths of Nature* (New York: Oxford, 1998), p. 151.

25. Tsonakwa and Yolaikia, *Legends in Stone, Bone, and Wood* (Minneapolis: Arts and Learning Services Foundation, 1986), p. 11.

26. Paul Gruchow, *Grass Roots: The Universe of Home* (Minneapolis: Milkweed Editions, 1995), p. 145.

27. As told to the author in conversation with Arnie Neptune (Grandfather Thunder), Penobscot elder, (Concord, MA, July 11, 2002).

28. Swami Prabhavananda, *The Song of God: Bhagavad-Gita,* trans. by Christopher Isherwood (New York: New American Library, 1951), p. 74.

29. Ray Berry, ed. *The Spiritual Athlete: A Primer for the Inner Life* (Olema, CA: Joshua Press, 1992), p. 139.

Index

A

Abram, David, 114–115
Ackerman, Diane, 106
administrators, 25–29
afterlife, 116
air pollution, 10–11, 99–100
air pollution tax, 11–12
alienation, 103, 106, 112
amnesia, moral amnesia, 100
Ancient Futures (NorbertHodge), 111
Andromeda galaxy, 85, 87–88
anemones, 108–109
Appalachia, 20, 23
Armchair Astronomy (Moore), 84
Arnold, Matthew, 100, 103
Artic National Wildlife Refuge, 6, 20
artificial selection, 63–65, 67
asthma, childhood asthma, 10–11
Auden, W. H., 22
Auriga constellation (Charioteer), 85–86

B

balance, compensatory ethic and, 18
  and death, 15, 114–115
  meditation for, 104, 105
  and nature, 106–108
  with resources, 110–113
  spirituality and earth, 109–110, 112
Bartholomew I, 108
Bauer, Grandpa, 43–44, 47
Beak of the Finch, The (Weiner), 64
bedrock sandstone formation, 39–40
Bennett, Gary, 82, 83
Berry, Wendell, 37, 112
Biblical references, 81, 93, 94, 108, 109
bicycles and development, 11–12
Big Bang theory, 81–82, 83, 84
"Big Flash, The ," 81–82
biophilia, 105–107
black holes, 84, 87
Blue Planet, The (Young), 88
Boötes Void, 79
boss (administrator) characteristics, 25–29
  and meadowlark values, 29
Brahman, 24, 116
Brownless, Donald, 90
Buddhism, 94, 110, 116
  See also Ladakh

C
Campbell, Joseph, 69
capitalism, 9–16
  and commercialism, 58–59,
    103–104
  and compensatory ethic, 10,
    18–19
  global economy and, 4, 102, 111
  natural (balanced) capitalism,
    15–16
  relationship to natural laws, 6, 9,
    12, 14
carbon, 82
carbon credits, 18–19, 99
carbon footprint, 18, 99
cars, 10–12, 99–100
Cassiopeia constellation, 87
children, 10–11, 20, 106, 115
Chinese religions, 80
Christianity, Holy Spirit and color
  yellow, 109–110
  See also Biblical references
Chung Tzu, 89
climate control, 18–19, 20
coresponsibility, 95, 97–104
  ecological footprints, 102–103
  and human consciousness, 116
  meditation on, 105
  modern life and, 103
  to shape actions, 100
CO_2, 10, 18–20, 99
coexistence, Leopold's "The Land
  Ethic," 17
  See also coresponsibility
colors of yin/yang. See flower
  meditation

Coma Berenices void ("The Hair of
  Berenice"), 79
commercialism, 58–59, 103–104
compensatory ethic, 12, 18–20
competition, 63–65
consumerism, 94–95
  and twoworlders, 112
consumers, 10, 19
  See also individuals
cosmology, 79–84
  modern, 80–81
craftsmanship, 22–24
creation stories, 79–81
creationism, 69, 71–72, 73, 81
  vs. myth, 73
cultural tradition, 110–113, 116
culture, 113
  and coresponsibility, 103–104
culturescapes, 111
Cygnus constellation (Swan), 86

D
Darwinian evolution, 63–64,
  71–73
death, 114–116
  and after death, 116
debt, and overabundance, Thoreau
  on, 51–52, 54
development, compensatory ethic
  and, 12, 19
  Thoreau on, 52–53
DeWitt, Calvin, 94
DNA, 105–106
Drucker, Peter, 25
Druyan, Ann, 72
Dying of the Trees, The (Little), 99

E

E =mc², 82

earth, human destruction of, 9–10, 20, 92–93, 95

humans, as interconnected with earth, 90–93, 95

interdependence with humans. *See* coresponsibility

spiritual and biblical commitment to, 93–95

earth (planet), 9, 71, 88, 90–92

ecosystem, prairies, 15

ecological consciousness, 12–13, 18, 93, 93–95, 104

man and role change, 17–18

ecological footprint, 102–103

ecology, capitalism and, 12–15

and cultural tradition, 110–113

and economics, 4, 6, 107

meadowlark values and, 4–6

spiritual practices and religions, 93–94

See also "Land Ethic"; political agendas

economics, and artificial selection, 63–65, 67

and capitalism, 9–10

and ecology, 4, 6, 107

and natural selection, 63

economists, job of, 3, 6–7, 17

economy, and coresponsibility, 3–4, 104

global markets and, 4, 102, 111

stability and balance, 111

Thoreau on, 51–52

Edsel automobile, 65

education. *See* learning; school

Eggert, Robert Sr., 22, 65

EIS (environmental impact statements), 6–7

elements, creation of, 82

endangered species, 5, 52, 59, 92, 94

Endangered Species Act, 94

environment, and pollution, 98–99

valuing and preserving, Thoreau on, 53

environmentalism, 20, 93–94

Erickson, Erik, 43

erosion, 41, 101–102

ethics, compensatory ethics, 18

greed, corruption, and politics and, 12, 14, 101–102

land ethics (Leopold), 17–18

workplace ethics, 29

evolution, 115–116

evolution of species, 63, 64, 66, 67, 91–92

extinction, 92

Exxon, 6

F

farming, 5, 19

fear, confronting fear, 46

finches (Galapagos Islands), 64, 66, 67

flower meditation, 105–116

cosmology and biological past (brown), 105–109, 114–116

cultural tradition (red), 110–113, 116

liberal learning (blue), 113–114,
  116
  spirituality (yellow), 109, 110, 116
folklore, 113
Ford Motor Company, 65–66
forests, capitalist values, 13, 101–
  102
  compensatory ethic and, 18–20
  ecological values of, 14
  logging and clear cutting, 6,
  13–14, 100–101
  pollutants and, 99–100
  sustainable yield management,
  13–14
fossil fuels, 5, 18–19, 20
free trade, 14, 102
future generations, 3, 6–7, 113–114

G
Galapagos Islands, 64, 66
galaxies, 83
Galileo, 71
gas, 11–12, 99–100
genetics, 115
GIS (grandchild impact
  statements), 6–7
glaciers, 39, 40
global ecology, 10, 18–19
global economy, 4, 14, 18–19, 102,
  111
globalization, effect of the West,
  111–112
Goodenough, Ursula, 115
government intervention, 9–10, 54
grandchild impact statements
  (GIS), 6–7
greenhouse gas emissions, 20,
  99–100

H
Hanh, Thich Nhat, 94–95, 99
health, healthy bodies and play, 43,
  44
  legislature and, 10–12
  and meadowlark values, 43
Herrigel, Eugene, 47
Hinduism, 94, 116
Holt, John, 31
Homo sapiens, 71–72, 73
human consciousness, 116
human evolution, 71–73, 90, 91,
  115–116
  natural selection and economics,
  63–65, 67

I
India's ecological footprint, 103
indigenous peoples and death, 114
  See also under individual cultures
individuals, coresponsibility, 3–4,
  20, 95, 98–100, 102–104
  and compensatory ethic, 20
  and life quality and simplicity,
  Thoreau on, 53–54
industry, 10, 18–19, 63–64
Islam, 110

J
Jesus, 94, 100, 108, 109
Judaism, 110
jumping, 43–47
Jupiter, 91

K
kinship, 110, 113–114
Kouroo culture, 23–24

L
Ladakh (India), 111–112
"Land Ethic, The" (Leopold),
    17–18
Lao Tzu, 105, 116
laws and legislation, 10, 12
learning, 31–35
  children and creation of topsoil,
    37–41
  instilling passion, 31–32, 33–35
  liberal learning, 113–114, 116
  passion for as goal of teaching,
    31–32, 35
  selflearners, 32–33, 35
Leopold, Aldo, 17, 107
life, 89–90, 110
  and death, 114–116
  earth's sustainability of, 90–92
  in ecosystems, 15–16
  meditation on, 105–106
lifestyle, and compensatory debt,
    20
  a simple life, 53–55, 94
  of today, 51–53, 54, 59, 103, 106
Little, Charles, 99
lobbies, 12
logging and clear cutting, 6, 13–14,
    100–101
loneliness, 106
Lyra constellation, 77

M
Macy, Joanna, 3
man, 17–18, 113–114, 115–116
martial arts, 46
materialism, 94, 95, 111–112
Mayan Quiche culture, 70

meadowlark economics, 6–7
meadowlark values, 5–6, 15–16
  teaching of, 31–32
  and Thoreau, 51, 53, 54–55
  See also *A Sand County Almanac*
    (Leopold)
meadowlarks, 5
meditation. *See* flower meditation
Menominee Indian tribe, 13–14
Merton, Thomas, 69
Milky Way galaxy, 84–87, 88
mindfulness, 105
Miracle Under the Oaks (Stevens),
    113
moon, 91
Moore, Patrick, 84
moral amnesia, 100
Muir, John, 97, 106, 107, 114
mushrooms, 89–90, 114
Mustang automobile, 65–66
Mustangs, The (Dobie), 66
mystical and spiritual states, 22, 23,
    45, 47
myths, 69–71, 73

N
Native American cultures, 69–70,
    80–81, 116
natural habitat preservation, 19
natural resources, balance and, 111
natural selection, and creationism,
    72–73
  early evolution, 91–92
  finches of Galapagos, 64, 66
  vs. artificial selection, 63–65, 67
nature, *biophilia*, 105–107
  effects of capitalism, 9–10, 52–53
  Thoreau on, 53, 57–59

Norbert-Hodge, Helena, 102, 111
North American's ecological
   footprint, 103

O
oil drilling, 6, 20
oil spills, 6
Orion constellation, 78–79, 85–86
overabundance and debt, Thoreau
   on, 51–52, 54
oxygen, 82
ozone pollution, 11, 99

P
Paiute Native Americans, 69–70
Philippines, 100–101
Phiny the Elder, 106
Physicians for Social
   Responsibility, 10
Pirsig, Robert, 22–23
plants, 39, 41, 109
plate tectonic, 91–92
Plato, 43
play, 22, 43, 44
political agendas, 12, 14, 101–102
pollution, and coresponsibility,
   98–100
pollution credits, 10, 18
power, 29, 32, 34
Power of Myth, The (TV series), 69
prairie ecosystem, 15–16, 113

Q
quality, 22–23
quasars, 83–84

R
rainforests, 14, 18–19, 101–102
Rare Earth (Ward and Brownless),
   90, 91
Raymo, Chet, 81–82
red spruce, 99–100
religions, Galileo and solar system,
   71
   and nature, 93–95, 104, 108–110,
   116
   religious tensions, 111–112
responsibility. See coresponsibility
rituals, 111, 113
Rolston, Holmes, 92

S
Sacred Depths of Nature, The
   (Goodenough), 115–116
Sagan, Carl, 72
Sagittarius constellation (Archer),
   86
schools, and coresponsibility,
   103–104
   current schooling system, 32, 59
   teaching meadowlark values, 31,
   32–35
   See also learning
Shadows of Forgotten Ancestors: A
   Search for Who We Are (Sagan
   and Druyan), 72
Sheehan, George, 44
Sirius constellation (Dog Star), 86
snail origins, 72–73
Snyder, Gary, 106
soil creation drama for children,
   37–41

solar system, 77–88
  location of, 84–85, 86, 87
"Song of Myself" (Whitman), 110
species, evolution, 63, 64, 66, 67,
  91–92
  extinction, 5, 59, 92–93, 94
spirituality, 93, 104
  meditation on (yellow), 109–110,
  112, 116
stars, birth and death, 71, 79, 82,
  83, 105
  See also under separate
  constellations
Stevens, Richard, 113
stock investments, 103
students, 32, 34, 35
sun, 71, 77, 78
  myths, 69–70
  Thich Nhat Hanh on, 94–95
Sun My Heart, The (Hahn), 94–95
Suzuki, D. T., 110

T
Tao, 89, 116
Tao Te Ching (The Way of Life)
  (Lao Tzu), 80, 93
Taoism, 105, 109–110
teachers teaching meadowlark
  values, 31–35, 32–34
technology, and craftsmanship,
  21–22, 23
  and meadowlark economics, 5
  negative aspects of, 52, 95, 113
  Thoreau on, 52–53, 58–59
Thelma (hurricane), 101, 102
Thomas, Del, 37

Thoreau, Henry David, 23, 51–55,
  57–61, 77, 106–107
  conversation with Thoreau in the
  modern world, 57–61
  debt and overabundance, 51–52,
  54
  meadowlark values and, 51,
  53–55
  on technology, 52, 58
topsoil, 100
topsoil drama, 37–41
trade, 4, 14, 102
tradition, cultural tradition, 110–
  113, 116
transportation, 12, 99–100
tree rental, 18–19
Tsonakwa, Gerald Rancourt, 21,
  116
two-worlder, 112, 113

U
UN Climate Conference (2007),
  18–19
universe, meditation on, 105–106
  origin of, 70–71, 78–79, 81–84
U.S. News and World Report, 10–11

W
Wal-Mart Pond, 57–59
Walden (Thoreau), 23–24, 51,
  52–55, 58, 106–107
"Walking" (Thoreau), 54
Walter, Mark, 92
Ward, Peter, 90
wealth, 55, 94, 103
Weiner, Jonathan, 63, 64

West, and effects of modernity on
   third world, 111–112
Whitman, Walt, 110
Whittier, John Greenleaf, 108
Wilson, E. O., 9, 106
Wisconsin, 11, 12, 39
wood flooring (lauan), 100–102
workplace ecology, 26–29

Y
Young, Louise, 88

Z
*Zen and the Art of Motorcycle
   Maintenance* (Pirsig), 23

About the Author

James Eggert is a writer and emeritus faculty member at the University of Wisconsin-Stout in Menomonie, Wisconsin, where he taught undergraduate students for thirty-three years. Eggert has written five other books including *What Is Economics* (fourth edition), *Invitation to Economics,* and *The Wonder of the Tao,* as well as articles and essays for journals and newspapers.

Eggert was a recipient of the university's outstanding teaching award, and for many years, advised the student environmental club, GreenSense. He currently serves on the town of Colfax plan commission and is a member of the Wisconsin Environmental Educators, as well as the Thoreau Society.

Eggert studied economics at Lawrence University in Appleton Wisconsin, served in Kenya, East Africa, with the U.S. Peace Corps (1964–1966), and later did graduate work in economics at Michigan State University. The author and his wife Pat have two adult children, Anthony and Leslie.